YOGA IN TEN LESSONS

YOGA IN TEN LESSONS

by

J.-M. DÉCHANET, O.S.B.

CORNERSTONE LIBRARY, NEW YORK

Reprinted 1969

CORNERSTONE LIBRARY PUBLICATIONS
Are Distributed By
Simon & Schuster Inc.
630 Fifth Avenue
New York, New York 10020

Manufactured in the United States of America
under the supervision of
Rolls Offset Printing Co., Inc., N.Y.

CONTENTS

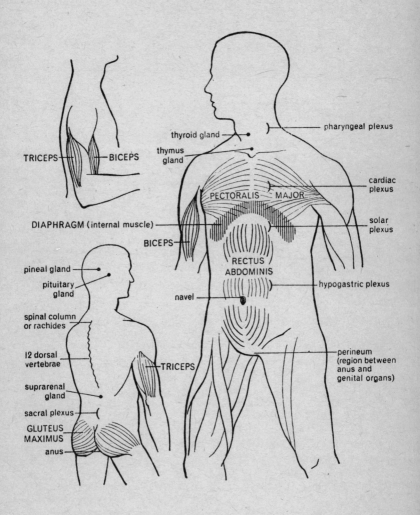

TRICEPS — BICEPS

thyroid gland

thymus gland

pharyngeal plexus

PECTORALIS   MAJOR

cardiac plexus

DIAPHRAGM (internal muscle)

solar plexus

BICEPS

RECTUS ABDOMINIS

navel

hypogastric plexus

pineal gland

pituitary gland

spinal column or rachides

12 dorsal vertebrae

TRICEPS

suprarenal gland

sacral plexus

GLUTEUS MAXIMUS

anus

perineum (region between anus and genital organs)

YOGA IN TEN LESSONS

INTRODUCTION

CHRISTIAN Yoga! Is it possible to develop a system of Yoga that is Christian in spirit? That is a question people have been asking for some years, and the answers given have been cautious in the extreme. It might be as well to have another look at them.

In a paper on "Yoga and the West"[1] Dr Jung observes that the European is so constituted that he "inevitably" makes the worst possible use of Yoga. Nevertheless he recognizes that some sort of Yoga, some form of Yogi discipline, is needed in the West. "Western civilization", he says, "must first of all be liberated from its narrow barbarism. If we are to succeed in doing this, we shall have to penetrate more deeply into what is properly human in man. This knowledge cannot be acquired by copying, 'aping', other people's methods, which came to birth in very different psychological conditions. The West will have to create its own Yoga, a Yoga built on Christian foundations – and in time it will do so."

These words of Dr Jung's are quoted by Fr Régamey, who goes on to say:

In time, yes! Unquestionably it will be a long-drawn-out affair. The architects of it will have to be Europeans: priests, religious and laymen, with a very strong and enlightened faith. They will have to be perfectly balanced

[1] "Le Yoga et l'Occident" in *Approches de l'Inde*, Cahiers du Sud (Paris, 1949), pp. 324-9.

personalities, at peace with themselves. While still young – round about thirty – they will have to sit at the feet of Mother India: some on the spot; others, if they can find a reliable *guru* there, in the West. All these conditions are really essential. Europeans who catch only a vague reflection of India, or those who assimilate her teaching, but lose their original characteristics in the process, are holding up the good work, not carrying it forward.[1]

M. Léon-Noël, a layman who devoted himself to Yoga on his own, without any help from anybody (so enthusiastically that he nearly lost his reason over it), says, writing after his conversion to Christianity:

An elementary knowledge of Yoga is certainly a factor making for physical and psychical balance. But if you want to progress beyond that stage you need a competent *guru*: a Christian *guru* if there is one, a master capable of leading his disciple on from Yogi methods of concentration to the prayer of adoration and contemplation before the presence of God. ... Yoga may help us perhaps to renew our methods of prayer; but I think – having been through it myself – that it first needs to be "converted", to forget itself and open its doors to the living God; it needs to recognize the freedom of the divine will, the divine person, as the centre of grace; in other words, to give up the idea of being an effective method of union with the divine. If we say that, if we call Yoga a method of paying heed to God that combines body and soul, then I believe in the possibility of not merely one, but many, Christian forms of Yoga.[2]

[1] *Vie Spirituelle* (August, 1955), p. 151.
[2] *Vie Spirituelle*, Supplément, No. 40 (1957), p. 125.

When these appreciations appeared, my own experience of Yoga was already under way. My aim was certainly a limited one. The idea of Christianizing Yoga – any Indian form of Yoga – was never in my mind. It was simply a question of making certain Yogi disciplines contribute to my own spiritual life. What I wanted to do, while remaining truly Christian, was to make something of myself, with the help of Yoga, in the sight of God, a personal and living God, the God of Revelation and the Bible.

I had read nothing of Jung, but I had come to the conclusion that a real, integrated Christian life could only start from a more profound conception of what was truly human in man. The immediate consequence would be a greater regard for man's nature, as willed by God; a great desire, too, to avoid separating in man what the Creator had, from the beginning, joined together. We are *body*, *soul* (mind) and *spirit* (heart). But in us the body and its inclinations too often dominate and overshadow the whole. Conversely, too often our aspirations go no further than an attempt to live on the intellectual plane. We seldom try to make the strength of our body and the triumphs of our reason serve the noblest part of our being – the heart, the spirit. Now it at once seemed to me that the Yoga exercises (the various postures [*āsanas*], and breathing exercises [*prānāyāmas*]) and the practice of concentration helped man to effect the synthesis, within himself, of the three aspects of his nature; to be at one with himself, to be himself in the sight of the God who created him and draws him perpetually to himself. It seemed to me that the Yoga exercises produced in us a certain silence favourable to contemplation, the approach of God and personal contact with the divine Persons. All I had to do was to decide on my aim, synchronize it with a thoroughly Christian ideal, and choose from all the Yogi exercises those which were most conducive to it.

I did not have to spend long at it. A sort of intuition came to my aid, and, after a few months of inevitable teething troubles (I had no *guru*!), I was able to put into perspective the experience I had gained, and all I have had to do since then has been to consolidate it. In 1955, at the request of Éditions Desclée of Paris, I wrote *La Voie du Silence*,[1] which was subsequently translated into many languages.[2] In the meantime, having been sent out to the tropics, and wanting to make the method known to people in Africa, both black and white, and being urged by many correspondents to explain more fully certain aspects of this method which had been set out in too concise a form in *Christian Yoga*, I prepared a complete correspondence course, the basis of this new book, in which I dealt once more with the essential points of the doctrine explained in *Christian Yoga*, setting out the Yogi postures and breathing exercises in a more instructive and progressive form.

It is this course, now carefully revised and adapted, that I have decided to publish in book form. I have retained the direct approach of the correspondence course and the same form of gradual initiation as regards both *theory* (basic principles and outlook of a Christian form of Yoga) and *practice*. The exercises have been increased in number. They are described in less summary fashion than in *Christian Yoga*, and in respect of each of them I have indicated the therapeutic effects and the attendant dangers, if any (*contra-*

[1] Desclée de Brouwer, Bruges-Paris, 6th edition, 1961.
[2] English translation, Burns and Oates, London, 1960, and Harper & Row, New York, 1959, under the title *Christian Yoga*.

indications). The book, which is, in effect, the product of numerous discussions with many disciples over the last six years, is complete with Notes and Explanations.

To tell the truth, I feel somewhat moved today at the thought of the welcome accorded in many parts of the world to my modest venture[1]. I see in this welcome an obvious proof of the need for a Christian Yoga, at all events a form of Yoga which is Christian in spirit. I hope my own experience will be of interest to others equally desirous of serving men and remaining faithful to the message of the living God and his Christ!

JEAN-MARIE DÉCHANET, O.S.B.

Monastère Saint-Benoît,
Kansénia (Katanga).

[1] The initial version bore the significant title: A Method of Contemplation based on Yoga.

Lesson One

WHAT IS HATHA-YOGA?

THEORY

THIS art, this system of integrated physical and psychical culture, is not easily defined. Its meaning, scope and purpose cannot possibly be made clear in a few words. The benefits of the system can best be realized by practice as they are gradually experienced.

Even at this early stage, however, I should like to give you an idea, necessarily incomplete but as accurate as possible, of *Hatha-Yoga* (which from now on I shall refer to as Yoga). For the moment, the best procedure would be to compare and contrast the exercises of Yoga with those of gymnastics and ordinary physical culture.

1. *Exercises with movement – exercises without movement*

Gymnastics develops the muscles by making them work. It subjects them to a certain number (sometimes a very large number) of alternate expansions and contractions, generally in fairly quick succession. For each muscle in the body there is one or more of these exercises.

Example: The following is one of many gymnastic exercises (commonly known as the *press-up*) for developing the triceps (muscles in the arm) and the pectoral and abdominal muscles:

Lie down with your hands flat on the ground and level with your chest. Push yourself up on your arms, keeping the body quite straight (Stretch). Then bend your arms till your chest touches the ground (Bend). Repeat both parts of the exercise ten, fifteen (or more) times running. Breathe in while stretching and out while bending (or vice versa).

Another example: to develop the abdominal muscles and also the muscles of the back:

Stand upright. Stretch your arms straight up above your head. Force the trunk back as far as it will go. Bend forward until you can touch your toes. Stand upright again. Repeat the exercise rhythmically until eventually you can place both hands flat on the ground – just for an instant.

This exercise does not lack grace. Once its purpose (touching the ground without bending the knees) is achieved, the only thing that counts is the movement. The whole attention is concentrated on carrying out the exercise as well and as quickly as possible, giving the maximum play to the muscles.

There is nothing like this in Yoga. In this lesson and the one that follows I am going to describe two Yogi exercises which can be compared with the physical culture exercises I have just detailed: in the *Snake*, there is the same stretching of the arms; in the *Deep Obeisance*, there is the same bending of the trunk. But in each case the exercise is done only once or twice – three times at the most – and each time slowly, as slowly as possible. Once the position has been taken up, it has to be held for a length of time – longer and longer each time.

Here, then, is the first difference (or rather, combination of differences) between gymnastics and the Yogi exercises. Let me sum them up:

1. Ordinary physical culture is exercise *involving movement*. Yoga is exercise *without movement*.
2. On the one hand: exercises *repeated* rapidly and vigorously, easy at first, but getting harder and harder. On the other: *one* position, always hard to take up; but taken up slowly and maintained for a more or less lengthy period.
3. In one case, a *succession* of contractions and expansions. In the other, a *single*, slow contraction of certain muscles, followed by a general relaxation.
4. In one case, the effort is mainly *muscular*. In the other, mainly *glandular* (as we shall see later).

Other and more important differences are concerned with the essential spirit of the two systems. They will be explained later. To be more precise, the more closely you follow my instructions the clearer they will become. But let me draw your attention to two of them.

2. *Gymnastic displays – gymnastics in private*

Ordinary physical culture lends itself to group-performance. It is spectacular, and the competitive element necessarily enters into it. When it is carried out by a group, success goes to the one who carries out the prescribed exercise the greatest number of times with the greatest agility. When the gymnast is on his own, he will strive to do each exercise better each time, better than the day before, and so on. This preoccupation is not perhaps unknown to the solitary Yoga enthusiast. But for him it does not have the same significance or carry the same weight. In Yoga the thing that matters most is *posture*. Students of Yoga take up their positions correctly, not by "jumping to it", but with grace. The spectacular side of the movements they carry out means nothing to them. Their attention is concentrated on their muscles at work, and then, having attained the correct position, they let go. They relax, and prolong their relaxation.

The student of Yoga is *on his own*; he must be alone to avoid distractions; to have the whole of his time to himself, to make the most of what peace and quietness there is.

Of course, the exercises can be carried out, for practice, in small groups under a fully-trained instructor. But it is better in general to work alone.[1] You work harder and get better results.

3. *Health, strength and beauty – Balance and self-control*

The essential difference between physical culture and Yoga lies in the objectives of the two systems. The gym-

---

[1] There is no reason why one should not arrange communal sessions from time to time. I envisage five or six adepts in the same town or community meeting regularly. The more experienced would take charge and arrange the postures according to a prearranged plan. The others would carry out the same exercises, but in complete freedom and each on his own account. This might last a quarter of an hour, or twenty minutes at the most. They would end with a "silent meditation" lasting at least ten minutes, each taking up the position he knew best (*Lotus, Perfect Posture* or its variants). There are two advantages to be gained from a session like this: the enthusiasm of the participants is renewed, and those who were losing sight of the purpose of the system regain it. The part of the man who takes charge at sessions of this kind is certainly not an easy one, but how rewarding! (See also, *Notes and Explanations*, section 1, p. 158 ff.)

nast's object is to make his body strong and healthy, with well-developed muscles, a broad chest and powerful arms. The Yogi will get more or less the same results; but they are not what he is looking for.

He is looking for calm, peace, the remedy for fatigue; or, better still, a certain immunity to fatigue.

He wants to quieten some inclination or other of his, his tendency to anger, or impatience – signs of disturbance in his organic or psychical life. He wants a full life, a more abundant life, but a life of which he is the master. He wants to escape the pressure of certain vital needs without losing the benefit of them. This is something we shall shortly see in detail.

What he wants, in a word, is to make the best of himself, and to get rid of the obstacles that stand in the way. His body, instead of being, as it so often is, a source of embarrassment, an obstacle to progress, to the impetus of man's intellectual and spiritual powers, must be a help to him.

I will not dwell at this stage on these vital questions. If you ask me the question: "How do the Yoga exercises manage to turn its devotees into calm, free, fully-developed men?" I shall reply: "Just wait and see. Start on the exercises, and by the time you are feeling the effects of the system I will explain all that to you. All that and much more!"

You know enough about it now to start certain exercises and some daily routines on your own.[1]

PRACTICE

How? When? Where?

The best place is the open air. Choose a really quiet spot, a bank by the river, a corner of your garden. Level the

[1] See also *Notes and Explanations*, section 1, p. 160.

ground, if need be; get rid of stones and twigs or anything that could hurt you or make you uncomfortable. Put down a mat or a rug.

But doing your exercises in the open is not always easy, or even possible. In that case you will have to fall back on your bedroom. It must be a quiet room, with plenty of fresh air. Put your rug down in a corner (the same one every time) facing the window.[1] Shut yourself in. It is important not to be disturbed. Never lie on your bed to do your exercises, unless it is a very hard one.

The best time is undoubtedly in the morning, before breakfast. Those who don't really feel up to it at that time of day can put off the session till they have a free moment. At night, just before bed-time, may be more suitable for them, as long as a certain time has elapsed since their evening meal. Better still, for people who work in an office, is the free time between their return home in the evening and their evening meal.[2]

Don't wear too much: bathing-trunks or a slip will do. You must be free in your movements. There must be no pressure on the waist or the stomach. Choose one of those exiguous slips that hug the top of the thighs.

First, learn to breathe

Breathing is important in ordinary physical culture. But in Yoga it plays a more important part still. You cannot

[1] Ideally, you should turn towards the East, facing the sun and in line with the axis of the earth's rotation.

[2] In the opinion of a Master (Selvarajan Yesudian), "it is not advisable to do the exercises just before going to bed, because the amount of oxygen absorbed during the breathing exercises and also the stimulating effect of the *asanas* (postures) have such an invigorating effect that it is difficult to get to sleep afterwards" (*Sport et Yoga*, Lausanne, 1961, p. 131). My own experience is just the opposite.

have any real Yoga without good breathing, breath-control and rhythmic respiration.

Breathing is quite an art. It is fair to say that most people do not know how to breathe. Certainly, few people pay any attention at all to their breathing at any time during the day. A good Yogi, on the other hand, reserves a few moments each day during which he makes a point of *following his breathing* and thinking about his breathing; a few moments during which, so to speak, he *breathes deliberately*.

Exercise 1: Abdominal breathing

Adopt a relaxed position.

Lie flat on your back on the ground; stretch out quite straight on your rug, feet slightly apart, arms at the sides or slightly away from the body (see which position you find most comfortable), palms preferably turned upwards.

Relax in body and mind. Look up. Let your eyes rest on some part of the sky or ceiling. At first, don't think about anything. Listen in complete detachment to the sounds that reach your ears.

After a minute or two, say to yourself: "I am going to breathe, slowly, as deep as I can." Or, better still, say quietly to yourself: "Take a good breath; a good, deep breath."

Then expel the air from your lungs, gently drawing in your stomach.

It will help if you place both hands flat on your abdomen without pressing. Gradually, as you expel the air, your hands will fall as the walls of your stomach subside.

To expel the air you half-opened your lips. Now close them, and breathe in gently through the nose. Imagine you are trying to fill, not your chest, but your stomach, with air. Your abdomen will rise again and push your hands up with it.

Then once more expel the air from your lungs and draw in your stomach.

I have stressed the points that are important: draw in the stomach when you breathe out. Breathe in through the nose (when you breathe out you can half-open your lips).

You will not manage to do this the first time. But tell yourself you will have to do it if you are going to succeed. "Abdominal" breathing, as it is called (because it makes you stick out your abdomen), is a characteristic feature of Yoga. You are not used to it. What you have been used to is breathing only "from the chest". You even try to "stick your tummy in", as they tell you in the army and in physical culture classes. So here is a difficulty to be overcome right at the beginning. But don't worry; you will overcome it. Later on in the course you will learn how to combine breathing from the abdomen with breathing from the chest. But one thing at a time. Never be in a hurry.

Another difficulty is breathing through the nose. You will get over this, too. Don't lose heart if your first attempts seem to get you nowhere. You cannot change old and ingrained habits in a few days!

Here, then, is your first major exercise.[1] You must breathe in and out, slowly and deeply, lying on your back, ten times.

[1] In *Christian Yoga* (p. 112), I recommend non-abdominal breathing for women. There is no reason to insist on this difference here. But women will always find it harder to breathe from the abdomen, and breathing from the chest, or the ribs, will always be predominant with them.

Exercise 2: The standing position

Being able to stand upright without getting tired is quite an art. Don't be surprised if I draw your attention in these early lessons to things that seem simple. "So that's what Yoga is all about!", you may say. Well, you will get to know more about it as we go on. You will grasp the importance of these movements and postures which are so simple in themselves but so difficult to take up correctly.

I am going to tell you one thing: you can relax, and relax very well, simply by standing on your feet. But you must get the position right.

Man holds himself erect (he is the only creature who can, and that is a sign of his natural dignity) when his joints fit into each other naturally; that is, by keeping his balance, observing the centre of gravity nature has given him. Man is particularly erect when the vertebrae of his spinal column (the axis of the human skeleton) take up the shape of the letter "S" – a shape clearly marked in the Congo women when they are carrying a load on their heads. My male readers might try it! Stand on your feet and imagine that you have to balance a bowl on your head. Stand quite still in that position. It will give you a feeling of well-being and relaxation.

The feet should be either parallel or at right angles, heels together or apart – there is no need to be rigid about this. Each of you will find instinctively the position that helps him to keep his balance best. Arms must hang down without being stiff, palms turned to the front or touching the outside of the thighs, towards the front. The stomach is flat, not held in or stuck out, or relaxed (look in a mirror).

If you take up this position you will soon get a feeling of well-being. You will get the impression that you can stay like that indefinitely without getting tired. In fact though, your natural tendency to "nerves" will very soon destroy the state of balance you have achieved; you will put one foot forward; you will move your arms; your head will droop; your backbone will sag and so on, and you will find yourself in an unsteady and tiring position, more exhausting than walking.

That is where the importance of this exercise comes in. *Remain* standing upright, as I have told you, *for some length of time*, immediately after the breathing exercise you did on your back. Stand like that for as long as it takes to breathe in and out fifteen times (a little longer than a minute: quite a time!) and concentrate on keeping *all your limbs still*. It's hard work, you will find. You will get pins and needles in your fingers. Keep at it. Gradually this natural position will become familiar to you, and you will begin to acquire a sense of balance, a rudimentary sense, it is true, but more practice during the course of the lessons will do much to perfect it and above all deepen it.

Exercise 3: The Snake (Phase One)

Lie down again, on your stomach this time, but do it like this:

Raise your arms high above your head; then bend the trunk slowly forward until you can place your hands quite flat on the ground, fingers in front, a good way from your feet. In this arched position, supported on your hands and toes, bend your arms and gently lower the body. Without strain (you push first one hand forward, then the other) your chest will come to rest on the ground, or rather on the back of your hands. Bend your head: your forehead must touch the ground. Stretch your feet well back, *soles turned upwards.*

Stay in this position for a moment. Relax. Breathe deeply, two or three times at least, drawing in the stomach as far as possible.

When you have established a feeling of deep peace within you, slowly raise the front of the body – from head to waist – by pressing on your hands and stretching the arms as far as they will go. The trunk takes the form of an

Fig. 1. "THE SNAKE" (Phase One)

arch, the head thrown back as far as possible. The lower part of the body, from the waist to the feet, remains in contact with the ground. The feet are stretched out in line with the legs (fig. 1).

As you raise yourself on your arms, breathe in deeply (through the nose).

Stay in this position as long as you can, with your arms stiff and your head back, holding your breath all the time. In practice, you will hardly be able to stay there a second, the first few times. You will gradually make it longer, but never use force.

Return slowly to the starting position (there are no

sudden movements in Yoga) by bending your arms. Once your head is touching the ground again and your chest resting on the back of your hands, start breathing again.

After a minute, go through the same exercise again. Do it three times running.

Therapeutic effects. This exercise has a well-nigh radical effect on hot-tempered young men and women by its action on the thymus. Also it assists the development of the personality. Apart from this, by getting rid of the stiffness of the spinal column it helps to develop the deep-seated muscles of the abdomen (the *rectus abdominis*) and the back. It makes the vertebrae work, especially the lumbar vertebrae. It has a very stimulating effect on the kidneys.

Contra-indications. There are none – except, perhaps, for people suffering from hypertrophy of the thyroid gland.

Exercise 4: *The Dolphin*

After a few minutes, take your head in your hands, with your fingers round the temples and the top of the forehead, and elbows and forearms resting on the ground. Then

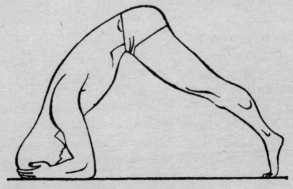

Fig. 2. "THE DOLPHIN"

slowly prop yourself up by raising the middle of your body and supporting it, partly on your forehead and elbows, and partly on the tips of your toes. Raise yourself right up and put one foot forward first and then the other, so that the line of your body forms an arc, as in fig. 2.

This position is relaxing. Hold it as long as you can. It is very good for abdominal breathing. You will have no difficulty in directing the air towards the lower part of the stomach and making the abdomen swell each time you breathe in. It will be just as easy to hollow your stomach when you breathe out.

So breathe in and out ten times in this position and concentrate on hollowing your stomach.

Exercise 5: The Kneeling Position

Now bend your knees. Keep your legs together, all the way down from your buttocks to your heels, as in fig. 3. Straighten up and sit lightly on your heels or between your heels. It is a little hard at first because of the stiffness of the ankles and the difficulty of keeping your soles uppermost. But, as they say, practice makes perfect.

Place your hands on your thighs or hold them together in front of your chest, fig. 4.

That is your first lesson. Carry out scrupulously the five exercises I have described every day for a fortnight, in the order in which they are listed here.

Fig. 3. "THE KNEELING POSITION" (Phase One)

Fig. 4. "THE KNEELING POSITION" (Phase Two)

You will notice that, beginning with Exercise 3, the different positions follow each other naturally You go from one to the other without changing your place, without making a single unnecessary movement. The whole set may take you a quarter of an hour. That's not very much. Of course, you can spend longer, if you like, in each position and on the rests in between. But before the fortnight is out you are going to feel some of the benefits of Yoga.

1. You are going to learn to breathe, or, more exactly, to recondition your breathing. If you take the trouble when you have some spare time during the day to practise some abdominal breathing, standing up, sitting down or lying down (in bed at night, for instance), you will feel a new life, a new vital force coming into you.

2. You are going to learn to hold yourself properly; to hold yourself better. I shall draw your attention to general bearing all the way through this book. The instructions given in Exercise 2 for standing still will, I am sure, mark the beginning of a great spiritual virtue in you, the virtue of stability. I shall be speaking about that again.

3. By practising Exercise 3, you are going to make the gland called the thymus (situated in the neck) work properly. You will be astonished, if you are a little highly-strung and hot-tempered, to find how much calmer you become. Perhaps you will get through the final week without losing your temper once. The same exercise will have its effect on the dorsal vertebrae and the intestines. It stretches them out, and from that you will get better digestion and a sense of lightness.

4. Exercises 4 and 5 are by way of preparation for other postures which are designed to bring you peace, to make a great calm descend on you. You will, perhaps, experience, right at the beginning, when you are on your knees and sitting back on your heels (the Carmelites' posture!), a general feeling of relaxation which makes the mind extremely lucid. That is the moment – you are a Christian – to breathe a prayer. . . .

Lesson Two

THE ORIGIN OF HATHA-YOGA

THEORY

YOGA is religious in origin. Thousands of years ago in India, some ascetics – monks of a kind – observed that certain positions of the body and certain methods of breathing were conducive to the life of prayer and contemplation to which they were dedicated.

They were not Christians. But like many races they sought God with all their hearts and wanted to be united with him, the Great First Cause as they called him, the great Power or Energy at work in the universe.

They professed the practice of "non-violence", that is, abstaining from all that could cause suffering to any living being; "truthfulness" – they abhorred lies and duplicity; "chastity"; and "poverty" – respect for the goods of others.

They cultivated "purity" – cleanliness of body and, above all, of heart. They wanted to be strong and happy, calm, even full of joy amid the difficulties of life. They were austere and tried to keep within certain limits of moderation on the physical plane (food, drink and sleep) and on the verbal and mental planes. They aspired to self-possession;

they wanted to control themselves, their bodies and their thoughts in order to get closer to God.[1]

A lofty and sublime ideal, and undoubtedly many of them attained it. Think of Mahatma Gandhi, who until quite recently was still practising their method. Think of Vinoba, who succeeded him!

In order to attain this ideal, to help them attain it, they had discovered a whole body of practices: *āsanas* (physical postures) and *prānāyāma* (breath-control). It is this system of practices that is called Hatha-Yoga.[2]

You are a Christian, just as I am. Then what, you will ask me, have practices invented by the adepts of a non-Christian religion to do with my life?

To that I shall reply: The Indians invented nothing. They merely discovered a universal principle, a phenomenon that holds good for any being made up of soul and body. This principle, this phenomenon, is the repercussion on the spiritual element in man, the soul (mind) and spirit (heart), of gestures and attitudes imposed on the body, the material element. They discovered, for instance, that by keeping the body still you calm the soul; that by stabilizing the body you help the mind to concentrate; by giving the body proper rest you help the mind to relax; by giving the body

[1] There is a name for each of these "aims" of Hindu Yoga – *yama* for the "abstinences", *niyama* for the "observances". An adequate description of them will be found in the article, "L'ancien Yoga et l'homme nouveau", which Fr Lambert (of the Discalced Carmelites in Bruges), who has lived for many years in India and practised Yoga under the direction of qualified masters, contributed to *Rythmes du Monde*, Abbaye de Saint-André, 1960, pp. 160–179.

[2] *Ha* means *moon*; *tha* means *sun*; *yoga* signifies a *joining together*. Hatha-Yoga is the art of joining together the "sun" and "moon" in man; in other words, creating harmony, in man, between the principle of material life (symbolized by the moon) and the soul or spirit, the principle of spiritual life (symbolized by the sun).

proper nourishment, making it absorb as much as it can of the vital energy contained in the air, the light of the sun and in water, you fortify the spirit; by seeing to the sound development of the body you enlarge the soul and make prayer and the search for God easier for it and more profound.

Do you not see from that how every man – and every Christian – can and ought to take part in that art which is called Yoga?

Priests and religious, men and women, make use of it, and benefits they gain from it are as striking as they are numerous.

One man was unwell. Having suffered from a long-drawn-out illness till he was nearly forty, he was suffering from the after-effects, always rather painful. In particular, he was subject to periodical fatigue, which took a long time to get rid of. Once he took up Yoga he saw the problems of general health which had bothered him in the past disappear, and fatigue for him become something rare. He does sometimes feel overtaxed, but all he has to do is to carry on with his ordinary exercises and he feels stronger again.

Another was highly-strung, hot-tempered, impatient for no reason at all. He is now much calmer. He no longer wants to take it out on others. Occasionally he loses his temper or raises his voice, but he soon calms down again.

Another man says he is stronger, more capable of endurance. He does more work and does it better. He enjoys good spirits and a pleasanter temperament. He is less upset than he used to be by life's little worries. Troubles he still has, but he faces up to them better.

Another man again has confided to me that the practice of certain virtues – chastity for instance – has become less difficult for him. On the intellectual plane, he finds he can cope with many things previously unknown to him. On the spiritual plane, prayer, a certain form of prayer, is particularly easy for him.

Yoga has so to speak made "more of a man" of these men, every one of them: men whose physical, intellectual and spiritual strength is more marked. It helps them to be better Christians. And all this because its disciplines, its practices, strange as they are to the uninitiated, are ordained for the balancing of that which makes each of us a man. By perfecting nature, they open up a way, as it were, one way among others, to the grace of the Almighty.

You are not an Indian; these priests, these religious I have spoken of, are not Indians. Like them, like you, I am a Christian, and a European into the bargain. Nevertheless, I have found it possible to make use of practices and methods imported from India to help me become what I am. But first (and this is the distinctive feature of the system of Yoga I am putting before you) I extricated them from the religious atmosphere which enveloped them in those parts, retaining only the kernel, the marrow, of use to all men, and transferred them to new surroundings in my own ideals and my life as a Christian.

You will now have a better idea of this Yoga, of which I gave you a brief description in Lesson One. I shall continue to unveil its secrets to you. Meanwhile, you are ready to embark on the second series of "manly" exercises.

PRACTICE

More air, more water, more sun

To grow, develop, get stronger, man must have constant recourse to nature for the energy his organism needs. That immediately makes you think of food ... and all the well-known vitamins contained in so many natural products that are so pleasant to eat.

But food is only one part of man's essential requirements, and a small part at that. There is *air*. You can live for days without eating; you can go for only a few minutes without breathing. Oxygen, which we take in at each breath, is "eaten" by the blood in the pulmonary alveoles and conveyed by it throughout the organism. The air we breathe in is life, strength coming into us.

Then there is *water*. The water we drink, the water we wash in. Drinking is as necessary as eating. It has been proved that a man can live with very little food, as long as he drinks water, lots of water. When we wash, the water does more than make us clean. The proof of that is the feeling of general well-being you get after taking a bath, a shower, or even just rubbing the body all over with a damp towel. Water takes away impurities, it is true; it promotes the circulation, true again; but it does more: it vitalizes. It causes a certain vital energy to enter into us.

Finally, there is the *sun*. It has been said that the sun nourishes. That is exactly what it does. At one time hardly anything was known about the sun, except that it gave out light and warmth and it burned. No one knew that the sun emitted multiple radiations and that solar rays were an active force. Today, everyone, or nearly everyone, knows about ultra-violet rays, the effects of which are so beneficial. A day in the sun, even if it is cold, gives a special boost to the organism. The sun nourishes.

What practical conclusions am I going to draw from that?

As far as the *sun* is concerned, I have no special advice to give you. I asked you in the first lesson to do your exercises in the open air if possible. No doubt it is only possible in exceptional cases. But try to arrange it if you can. You should choose a time when the sun is well up without being too hot; a time when its rays are not too oblique or in danger of being reflected by the layer of (invisible) mist covering the ground, i.e. returned to the sky as if by a mirror. Not too late in the day, therefore, and not too early either! I am thinking of those who live at the seaside or in the hills. Ten or eleven o'clock in the morning seems to be an excellent time. The head should be protected, with the sun shining on the greater part of the body. The first lessons last only ten minutes. The novice is in no danger of sunstroke! Before the course is over he will be quite used to bright sunlight and be able to stay out in it for hours. Those who live in towns, or down in the plains, should not miss any opportunity of taking a sunbath. Perhaps the room in which they do their exercises is well situated and the sunshine comes flooding in? Let them take as much advantage as they can of the soothing effect of the ultra-violet rays.

Water. If you have a suitable opportunity of settling down by the side of a river or a stream, or near a waterfall, even if only once in a while, take advantage of it. The way to start is to take a refreshing dip. Plunge into the water with the sun shining on it; get right under the waterfall. The minute you are dry, start on the breathing exercises and the postures. If the water is fit to drink, take a few long draughts of it. There is energy in this sun-drenched water. Those who do their exercises in the bedroom can moisten the body with a face-flannel or a towel before and after the exercises. They too should drink, slowly, a few mouthfuls of water.

Air. I told you to wear as little as possible: that was because it is important that your skin should be well aerated during your exercises. After a time, you will feel the need to get rid of anything that gets in the way. Don't forget to open the window in the bedroom!

A. BREATHING

Exercise 6: Rhythmic breathing

During the last fortnight you must have got into the way of breathing from the abdomen. You should be able to make your diaphragm drop when you breathe in and rise again when you breathe out just by thinking about it. But if you haven't got to that stage yet, don't despair: have another go at Exercise 1; do it several times a day.

At all events, take a step forward now: learn how to make your breathing *rhythmic*.

Lie flat on your back, as for Exercise 1, or stand on your feet (Exercise 2). Take your pulse. Each beat of the heart represents one unit. So without bothering about anything else count 1, 2, 3, 4, 5 up to 10 or even 20. What you have to do is to get into the same rhythm as your heart and make it the basis for your breathing. You will soon get the idea.

Now pull your stomach in, at the same time expelling the air through the mouth. Then close the lips and breathe through the nose, counting mentally 1, 2, 3, 4, in time with the beat of your heart. Breathe out again right away, counting in the same way 1, 2, 3, 4. Repeat the exercise five times at first and later on ten times.

If you don't manage to do it perfectly, don't get excited about it. That is quite normal. I should be surprised if you were successful the first time. You will have some failures.

But you will gradually get into the way of it, and, once you have got the habit, it will be like a game for you, an amusement, to breathe in time with your heart.

1, 2, 3, 4 – 1, 2, 3, 4 ... I don't think it will be more than a few days before you feel that this is doing you good.

If you find you are getting a bit out of breath, cut it down a little. Change the rhythm to 1, 2, 3 – 1, 2, 3. But you must manage to slow down progressively and get into the rhythm, for instance, of 1, 2, 3, 4, 5 – 1, 2, 3, 4, 5 (from now on I shall indicate this rate by the figures 5–5) or even 6–6. This rhythm, 6–6, is the one I have reached myself. It is *my* rhythm. You too will discover your own rhythm. And you must stick to it. It will be a real game, I repeat, a pleasure for you, breathing like this.

B. POSTURES

Exercise 7: The Deep Obeisance

Once you have finished your five or ten breathing exercises, get up again (if you were lying down) without any sudden movements.

Stand to attention, but without any stiffness. Contract the muscles of the thighs, hold your hands together in front of your chest, then raise your hands above your head, breathing in, slowly and deeply, all the time, so as to form a sort of arch with your arms, which should be touching your ears. Stretch out to your maximum height. This is the first phase.

Stay like that for a few seconds, *holding your breath*. Then, open your arms slightly, keep them stretched right out and bend forward slowly in a curve, breathing out all the time.

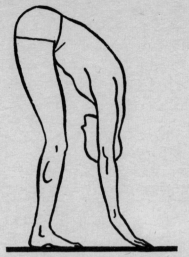

Fig. 5. "THE DEEP OBEISANCE" (Phase One)

Try to put your hands quite flat on the ground, some distance away from your feet (second phase).

Don't stay in this arched position, with your hands on the ground, more than a moment. Return to your original position, breathing in deeply all the time. Let your arms fall to your sides. Breathe out (third phase).

You may feel a bit giddy at first.

The second phase is fairly hard, but you are young. Besides, even if you are old (or infirm in some way) and cannot manage to touch the ground with the flat of your hands, it doesn't matter. It is the effort that counts. The great difficulty is keeping your legs straight. You will find it difficult at first, if not impossible, to avoid bending them. Look at the illustrations.

Figure 5 shows how the *Deep Obeisance* is done by a beginner, but one who is getting on quite well. He has made

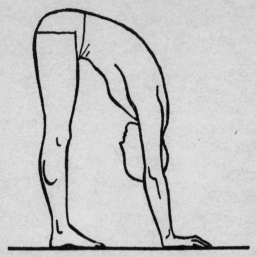

Fig. 6. "THE DEEP OBEISANCE" (Phase Two)

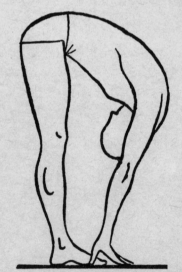

Fig. 7. "THE DEEP OBEISANCE" (Phase Three)

the mistake of trying to place his hands too near his feet. His legs are bent.

His colleague (fig. 6) is going about it more carefully: he has made his head swing forward a bit and his hands are placed some distance (twelve inches) from the nearest point of his feet. In time he will get them nearer. Perhaps he will even manage to get his hands on either side of his feet, with his head hanging right down till it is almost, if not quite, touching his knees (fig. 7). But this is quite a performance, not permissible for novices of Hatha-Yoga (with certain exceptions, of course).

However things go, don't use force. Don't worry too much about making mistakes.

Therapeutic effects. They scarcely need emphasizing: the spinal column becomes more supple; the muscles of the legs, abdomen and thighs become stronger.

Contra-indications. There are few. People suffering from displacement of the spine will naturally exercise care, without necessarily abstaining from the exercise.

At the beginning, I would advise you to do three *Deep Obeisances* (first, second or third phase). Take care to breathe rhythmically (three or four times) between each of them. The third phase is linked with the exercise called the *Snake*. I say "linked" advisedly. The great thing is to pass from one exercise to the next, quite naturally, without a break. This is made possible by the use of intermediate exercises; we will see how these are done now so as to be ready for them when the time comes.

Exercise 8: Intermediate postures

In the second phase of the *Deep Obeisance* you are bending right down. Keep your hands quite flat on the ground and move your right leg back as far as you can. Then bend the left knee. This will bring your chest to rest against your thigh. Then move your left leg as far back as possible. As you do this, lift up your head.

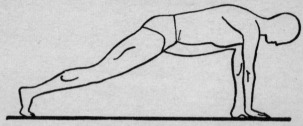

Fig. 8. "INTERMEDIATE POSTURE"

Next, push your body forward, pivoting yourself on your hands and toes.

This will make your chest jut out in front of your arms; first your knees, then your thighs and finally your stomach

Fig. 9. "THE SNAKE" (Phase One)

will touch the ground. Your feet, instead of forming an acute angle, will now describe an obtuse angle (fig. 9).

Finally your chest itself comes to rest on the ground

between your two forearms. You are now in the starting position for the *Snake* posture (Phase Two) which I am now going to describe to you.

See figs. 8 and 9 for the two intermediate postures which make it possible to link the *Deep Obeisance* with the posture that follows.

Exercise 9: The Snake (Phase Two)

This time your forearms are not under the chest, as in Exercise 3, but on each side of it.

With your face on the ground, take several deep breaths and then slowly raise the front part of the body, supporting it on the hands and forearms. A glance at fig. 10 and another at fig. 1 (the *Snake*, Phase One, p. 24) will make the difference between these two postures clear.

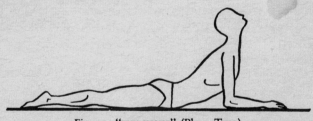

Fig. 10. "THE SNAKE" (Phase Two)

Remain for a second (at first: you will extend this period later) with arms outstretched, holding your breath all the time. Then return to the starting position while breathing out completely.

Repeat the exercise up to three times. Try not to rely on your arms. It is the whole trunk that has to make the effort, especially the dorsal vertebrae. Close them up, as if they were the hinges on which your spine turns. Pull on your stomach. Hard? A bit harder than Exercise 3, but then we are getting on.

Obviously the therapeutic effects mentioned in Lesson One (p. 25) are more marked here. It is a good idea, nevertheless, to do the two methods alternately, as they are complementary to each other.

Exercise 10: The Dolphin

This is the same as Exercise 4, without any modification. But when you breathe, breathe in and out completely, and when you breathe out, give yourself the impression that the muscles of the anus or the perineum are trying to meet the navel.

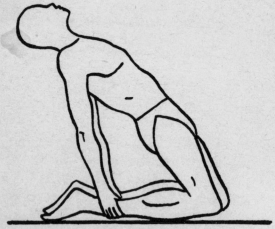

Fig. 11. "THE HALF BACKWARDS BEND"

Exercise 11: The Half Backwards Bend

As you did after the *Dolphin*, in Lesson One, bend the knees and raise the trunk. But stay on your knees without sitting back on your heels.

Arch your torso backwards and throw your head and shoulders back. At the same time take hold of your ankles with your hands. Get your head well back; look up at the sky or the ceiling (fig. 11). The more arched the trunk the better the position. The angle made by the legs and thighs must be as wide as possible. The object is to stretch the muscles of the abdomen and the internal organs as well as to make the spine more supple.

Later on, we shall drop this posture in favour of a more difficult and more efficacious one – the *Full Backwards Bend*.

Fig. 12. "THE FOLDED LEAF"

Exercise 12: The Folded Leaf

Now here we have a posture of relaxation.

Let go of your feet; straighten the torso. Sit back on your heels or even between your heels. Lean forward: your head should be near the ground, or even touching the ground, so that your nose rests between your knees. Get your arms right back with the back of your hands on the ground.

Now you are folded in three and relaxed, you should have a feeling of well-being all the more marked on account of the extra effort put into Exercise 11. Make this relaxation last as long as you like. What peace when you get up again; what a feeling of renewal!

Exercise 13: Preparation for the Perfect Posture

This lesson ends with an exercise in preparation for one of the most difficult postures in Yoga: the position called the Perfect Posture. This is a method of sitting down with the legs folded, and it gives a feeling of relaxation and satisfaction. It is a difficult position for a European to take up, because Europeans are not trained to it from infancy as Indians are. It takes weeks and months of persevering effort. Once the result is achieved you are richly rewarded for your trouble. We will begin by establishing the preparatory exercise for the Perfect Posture.

Sit down on the ground with your trunk quite straight. Keep your legs as far apart as you can.

Then fold the left leg, and with the help of your hands place the sole of the foot against your right thigh, with the heel as near as possible to the fold in the groin. Now try to keep your left knee on the ground (fig. 13).

That is the difficulty. If you think it will help, you can slip a little cushion, or better still a rolled-up rug, under your seat, towards the back. Supported in this way, you will find it more comfortable to keep your left knee on the ground.

You can also place your heel under the perineum (in which case the rug is indispensable). This brings your foot almost entirely under your right thigh. That is a little harder. But some people very much prefer this way of doing it.

This is only a preparation. Later, you will practise placing the right foot on the left leg: or rather, between the left leg and the left thigh, with the left foot remaining in place alongside the right thigh. The difficulty then will be to keep the right knee on the ground. It is difficult! But you get there in the end. . . .

Fig. 13. "THE PERFECT POSTURE" (Preparation)

Lesson Three

WHAT DOES HATHA-YOGA LEAD TO?

THEORY

A BETTER BALANCE IN MAN

In Lesson One, I touched on the admittedly difficult subject of the *object* of Yoga. I returned to the subject in Lesson Two, in which I pointed out what it had done for certain of its adepts. Today I want to tell you in more explicit fashion where these exercises I am suggesting for you are leading. It has always seemed to me that Yoga aims at:

1. A better balance in man.
2. Calm and peacefulness.
3. A certain development on the natural plane.
4. Finally (since it is Christian Yoga and a Christian spirit we are concerned with) a greater involvement in the sphere of Christian life.

What are you? A man? Are you quite sure? You really feel yourself to be a man?

I do not think it will take you more than a few minutes' reflection to admit, without any mock-modesty, that, taking everything into account, you are not really a man *yet*, or else you are not the man you were: you do not feel that you are yet fully developed.

Man, a man, is not just that creature who stands upright,

with a harmoniously-proportioned body, a melodious voice, bright eyes, skilful hands, all mixed up with the beasts of the field which he dominates by his wits. Man, this masterpiece of God, this lord of creation, is a being who in his acts as well as his thoughts manifests something great, strong and superior which we call *virility*.

A fine body and powerful muscles are not enough to make a man (Latin = *vir*).

An enlightened intelligence, quick wits and a sensitive heart are still not enough to make a man.

There must be a power indwelling in each of these elements – a power that we call health in the body, character in the soul, elevation in the mind and constancy in the heart. The vitality of each of these needs to be balanced and harmonized. The activity of one of them must not become an obstacle or a barrier to the development of another.

For instance, the impetus of certain desires which have their seat in the depths of the heart must not be broken, or even weakened, by the attraction of other desires originating in the body or the mind; the development of the intelligence must not be held back or brought to nothing by weakness, whether it is physical (illness) or psychical (lethargy, lack of will) or moral.

It takes a lot to make a man[1] and you all feel, and observe, that something in you is missing if you are going to be what you should be. You meet obstacles every minute of the day to the fully-developed life you aspire to.

A man I know is ill. To be more exact, he is "poorly". In other words, he is troubled by a complaint that is

[1] It is obvious that what is said about *man* applies equally to *woman*. There is a certain *femininity*, and even a certain *virility* – in the psychic sense – about women, of which the perfect type is the "vigorous wife" of Proverbs 31. 10.

admittedly not very serious, but enough to clip his wings. Ill-health has become translated in his case into loss of energy and lethargy.

Others, without being infirm, are saddled with little weaknesses, congenital for the most part. These come under such headings as bad temper, irritability, manias of one kind or another, neuroses, pessimism, masked pride, shameless desires, secret impurity.

Almost everyone lacks vitality, energy, character. Everyone stops half-way on the road to manhood.

What we must understand about these various *diseases of the soul* – fruits, like death and illness, of original sin—is that they are sometimes, indeed quite often, linked with physical deficiencies, with a sometimes complex lack of balance in the organism. In such cases, the stomach, the liver, the nerves, the internal secreting glands (pituitary, thyroid and suprarenal) are more to blame than the spiritual organism, the heart, the soul or the conscience. The way to remedy the defects of the soul is to look after the body, block the road to certain desires and prevent deviations. The intelligent care of the body – in moderation – will give vitality to the soul and the spirit as well.

And that is the object, the main object, of Yoga: to stimulate and balance certain physical functions in order to liberate and develop spiritual energy. To make man a "virile" being, with all that that implies.

A. Stimulation of bodily functions

The first concern of the Yogi is, as we have seen, to learn how to breathe properly. On the physiological plane respiration plays a fundamental part. To live is to breathe; to breathe properly is to live better. Slow and thorough breathing can transform a man in a few days. Why? First, because it activates the oxygenation of the blood. By this means it promotes, at one and the same time, the regeneration of pure cells and the elimination of toxins (waste matter secreted internally). It facilitates the circulation and makes it more regular. Hence there is a relaxation of the heart, relief of congestion in certain organs and a general warming up of the system. I shall return to these phenomena later.

There is one indirect effect of proper breathing that must not be overlooked: the kind of breathing I described on page 20, breathing from the abdomen, makes the diaphragm work. When you breathe in, this membrane falls and massages the intestines. This gives you a better functioning of these organs and the radical suppression of one of the chief factors making for poor health – constipation.

This, you will say, is not the real purpose of Yoga. I agree. But since Yoga is a first-class school in the matter of respiration, I had to make clear to you at the very beginning its therapeutic action in this connection.

Note also that the postures, or *āsanas* as they are called, help the respiratory rhythm to promote the circulation. But first and foremost their sphere of influence is in the glands known as endocrines, the glands that secrete hormones, and their action on these has been proved to be efficacious.

At the critical age of puberty a posture like the *Bent Bow* (Lesson Four) can accelerate the maturing of the sexual glands and restrain the atrophy of the thymus (the gland of growth, situated at the front of the neck) at the same time. The thymus gradually disappears as the sexual glands develop. It must not disappear too quickly, however, since the correct development of the human body depends upon it. A dwarf is one whose thymus has atrophied too quickly; a giant is one whose thymus has not retired soon enough. In both cases, exercises like the *Bent Bow*, the *Snake*, the *Half Backwards Bend* and the *Full Backwards Bend* are of a kind to provide a remedy. Such exercises can also regularize defective growth (too quick or too slow).

They act in the same way, and in radical fashion, on the thyroid, the gland whose two lobes, on each side of the larynx, are perceptible to the touch. Like the thymus, and to a greater degree, the thyroid presides over physical and intellectual development in man. When a child is born without a thyroid, or with a degenerate thyroid, he remains abnormal; he is what we call a *cretin*. The young man whose thyroid is insufficiently productive becomes lazy: he lacks character and temperament. A few *āsanas* done well, and the "virilizing" action is clear. Slowly, perhaps, but all the more surely, he acquires energy and a readiness for thought and action of which he never thought himself capable. These postures have stimulated the activity of the thyroid.

Others, like the *Deep Obeisance* (Lesson Two), the *Back-stretch* (in this Lesson) and the *Plough* (Lesson Five), will have a therapeutic effect on the digestive organs. They stimulate the activity of the liver, the stomach and the kidneys. Others again, by acting on the nervous system as a whole, will generate courage, virility and self-confidence.

B. *Better balance*

Most physical disorders like feebleness, giant stature or dwarf stature, and mental disorders like laziness, lethargy, apathy or despondency, have their origin in inadequate secretions of one or other of the endocrine glands. Over-production can also be implicated. When the thyroid

overproduces, the iodine it secretes passes into the organism, excites the nerves and increases the blood pressure.
This gives rise to agitation and, what is worse, irritability.
What a lot of Yoga novices have been in a position to write
to me after a week of exercises to say that they "no longer
recognize" themselves. Their irritability had simply disappeared. Two or three exercises were enough to regularize
the thyroidal secretion and combat one of the factors
making for organic disorder.

To a young man in search of sexual equilibrium, we can
say:[1] "Take up Yoga! First, the exercises will distract you
from all this sex that bothers you. And then, simply by
relieving the congestion in the parts concerned, they will
lead to the gradual disappearance of temptation. For the
mastery of chastity from the moment of puberty there is
nothing to touch the *Pole* and *Plough* postures. Finally, by
the same balancing effect they have on the whole organism
such *āsanas*, combined with a moderate rhythm in breathing,[2] will implant in you that virility which is just the
complete opposite of sexual psychosis."

In the next lesson we shall deal with other complexes,
other troubles. Today you have learned that man is a being
in whom different kinds of life, different planes of life, are
linked to each other and, as it were, interdependent. The
adage rightly says: "A healthy mind in a healthy body";
which must be interpreted: "Look after your body
in order to heal your soul". We have not always seen
things in this light. There was a time when looking after
the body or "cultivating" the body appeared to be an

[1] See Notes and Explanations (Appendix I), section 2, p. 162.
[2] I say "moderate" because all excess, all haste, may have the opposite
effect!

irregular procedure, incompatible with the true Christian life, the life called spiritual. The cultivation of the body can certainly be wrongly understood. It can turn into the *cult* of the body, which is wrong. Cultivating the body is not an end in itself. As Max Marin has aptly said: "The body must be sanctified while it is being cultivated".[1] And *this* is the object of the system of Yoga I am putting before you.

PRACTICE

A. RESPIRATION

Exercise 14: *Holding the breath*

Rhythmic breathing is by now familiar to you. Now

Fig. 14. "THE TREE" (Phase One)

[1] In his book: *L'Athlète Chrétien*, which appeared in Brussels in 1944 and deserves a new impression.

we go a stage further. What we have to do is to insert, between breathing in and breathing out, a period when you hold your breath. So count, as in Exercise 6 – 1, 2, 3, 4. Then hold your breath while you count 1, 2, or better still, 1, 2, 3, 4, and then release your breath, counting all the time in the same rhythm 1, 2, 3, 4. If it will help, you can hold your nose for the required interval after breathing in.

You will improve gradually and get to the rhythm 6–6 mentioned earlier. Do all this steadily, without strain or fatigue.

B. POSTURES

Exercise 15: The Tree

This is what is called a balancing exercise. If you are not already perfectly balanced, you will have some difficulty in doing it and especially in maintaining the position. That is a sign that you need it badly. Your efforts will be all the more persevering. The *Tree* will give you something you lack: stability, balance.

Stand up straight, with your arms falling naturally alongside the body. First take the weight of the body on the left leg. Then lift the right foot and take hold of it with your hand; slide it up the leg till it fits into the lower extremity of the left groin. Lean heavily with your toes on the fleshy part above the knee so that the foot does not slip.

Straighten up, and hold your hands together in front of your chest. See fig. 14, which clearly indicates the position of the foot, leg and hands.

If at first you don't manage to balance on your left foot, stand next to a piece of furniture or a tree so that you can support yourself against it. You will have some failures. Do not lose heart. Start again. On certain days it is more difficult. Physical fatigue and especially mental fatigue bring about this lack of balance in the organism, which expresses itself in the instability of the body and the need to move.

Stand still for a moment with your hands joined together. Breathe normally several times, looking straight in front of you. Then raise your arms, keeping your hands together, so as to form an arch over your head. Hold your breath (you have naturally been breathing heavily as you raised your arms, as you do, and always will do, whenever you

Fig. 15. "THE TREE" (Phase Two)

stretch) for a few seconds. Then breathe out gently, at the same time bringing the hands back in front of the chest or slowly allowing your arms to resume their original place at the side of the body. Replace the right foot on the ground. Take another breath and start again with the other foot.

It is a little difficult, but how beneficial!

The *Tree* posture is susceptible of many variations. For instance, once your arms are raised, you can keep them apart and throw the head and shoulders back. Or instead of raising them you can cross them at the back, level with your shoulder-blades. Later we shall come to more difficult variations.

Therapeutic effects. The *Tree* posture calls for no contra-indications. It has a calming effect and promotes the proper working of the nervous system.

Exercises 16 and 17: The Deep Obeisance and the Snake

Now combine the two exercises I have described to you in the preceding lesson. Add to them the *Dolphin* and, if you like – every other day, for example – the *Kneeling Position* as well. After which you sit with your legs stretched out in front of you and your trunk quite straight.

Fig. 16. "THE BACKSTRETCH"

Exercise 18: The Backstretch

From the sitting position, raise your arms as high as you can above your head. Then slowly bend forward, breathing out completely and drawing in the stomach. Grip the toes with the fingers. Pull hard on them and use them to lever yourself forward so that after quite a lot of practice you should be able to make your forehead touch your knees. But the main thing is to stretch the muscles of the back and especially the spine. After a few seconds (you will gradually improve on this), stop holding in your stomach and breathe in vigorously but slowly. At the same time sit up again and raise your arms in a gesture of relaxation.

Repeat up to three times. Then lie down with your arms alongside your body and relax, breathing just as you like.

This exercise calls for some effort. You will not manage to get your head anywhere near your knees the first time, nor for a long time afterwards. Tell yourself that it doesn't matter. It's the effort that counts. It is more important to make sure that your legs and thighs are kept stretched right out.

Therapeutic effects. The exercise is excellent for the muscles that control the abdominal organs and for the pelvis. It is of inestimable value for any deficiency of the liver or kidneys. It relieves congestion in certain organs and at the same time irrigates the prostate and the sexual parts. It restrains the lower appetites. If carried out before going to bed, it allays erotic desires or makes them disappear.

Contra-indications. There are few postures which call for absolute contra-indications; at the most, they call for counsels of prudence and moderation. Thus, the *Backstretch* should be taken up cautiously by people with spinal trouble; similarly, those who are affected by functional disorders of the liver, stomach, spleen, kidneys or intestines. Yoga exercises generally have the effect of preventing these disorders rather than curing them. It is none the less true that in cases of this kind their therapeutic effects remain powerful. Caution does not imply abstinence! The man who is poorly, the man who is ill, will take things slowly, and gradually improve.

Fig. 17. "THE HALF-CANDLE"

Exercise 19: *The Half-Candle*

What I am suggesting to begin with is more like half a candle! Once you are relaxed, raise your legs, thighs and buttocks, supporting them by slipping your hands under them. (It may help you, at first, to use a thick, hard cushion to support them.) Get your legs higher still, until they appear above your eyes or even farther back. If necessary, raise your seat still higher; the object is to achieve a definite feeling of balance and well-being. Breathe normally. Keep your attention concentrated on your circulation. For instance, follow the path taken by the blood, the passage of which – through the veins of your legs, thighs and trunk – this exercise greatly facilitates. It is indeed one of the great benefits of the exercise, and it considerably reduces the work of the heart. You can go on with it indefinitely. It has no contra-indications.

End up by lowering your seat and bringing your legs down again. Remain lying down for a few minutes and concentrate on your breathing.

Lesson Four

WHAT DOES HATHA-YOGA LEAD TO?
(*Continued*)

THEORY

TOWARDS CALM AND PEACE

"It would be a misunderstanding of the unity of the human being to suppose that spiritual realities such as temptations, sins or virtues are disembodied events taking place only in the soul. They are undoubtedly, as we shall have occasion to repeat in even stronger terms, far more than manifestations of bodily activity, and it would be a most serious mistake to degrade mental life to the level of physical phenomena. At the same time we should be guilty of a disastrous and vicious form of presumption if we overlooked the share of the flesh – by which we mean the totality of the visceral functions – in our good or bad moods, our generosity or selfishness, our courage or cowardice.

"Since then, in the already quoted words of St Thomas, 'greatness of soul results from a sound bodily constitution', we are under an obligation, if we wish to acquire or retain moral self-control, to take care of our health: physical fitness becomes a 'duty'."[1]

This quotation from a doctor well known in the scientific world will help you to understand what I said in the

[1] René Biot, *What is Life?* (London and New York, 1959), pp. 85–6.

previous lesson. It may remove any remaining doubts about the part played by the body in our moral life which I was speaking about in that lesson; about the need to care for and cultivate one's body in order to influence the soul.

I told you that this combination of qualities, this *virility* that makes us what we are, is linked with the proper functioning of certain glands in our bodies. To stimulate these glands and keep their secretions in balance with each other is to take a step – a big step – towards virile energy. This is the first objective of the system of Yoga I am putting before you. But this is not all. Yoga takes us further.

We find it very difficult to be ourselves. We are very sensitive, very easily moved. We can be moved, or disturbed, by almost nothing. More often, our nerves are put to the test by events and things that happen. To live is to consume energy, to make a continual effort. It is to be "in travail". And this travail is fatiguing, exhausting, wearing. We are losing energy the whole day through. We are emptied of all our strength. The Creator has fittingly provided for repose to enable our organism to recuperate these vital powers engaged in the daily round, to give relaxation to our nervous system, that work, both physical and mental, has little by little overexcited. Alas, nightly repose is often no more than a word. Sometimes sleep just won't come; and even when it does it is often not a sound sleep. The dawn finds us in scarcely better condition than when we went to bed the night before. And all the worries, all the cares that were on our mind yesterday, are with us again today. We start off again courageously, but tired and enervated. At the first shock our reserves, stretched to breaking point, give out altogether. In the circumstances this is not surprising.

Hatha-Yoga gives repose, calm and peace both to the body and the soul: the whole human complex. It soothes the nerves, eliminates fatigue, helps us to recuperate our lost strength, recharges our organism up to the hilt, drives away worries and finally clarifies our ideas. It enables man to find himself again after he has given himself to others. The facts are there. How can they be explained?

In order to understand it, let us see what a Yogi does, how he lives. At the time of day when keep-fit addicts devote ten minutes or a quarter of an hour to their daily dozen (exercises in the bedroom, a brisk walk, breathing exercises, followed by the traditional shower) the Yogi carries out a whole series of exercises at a slow, deliberate pace, and he does them with movements which are neither more nor less comical or extravagant than those of the physical culture exercises familiar to the West. Another important point is that the Yogi maintains each posture for a few seconds, or minutes, depending on the particular exercise. He stands upright, with his arms stretched to the limit above his head; then he bends forward, without any abrupt movements, keeping a firm rein, as it were, on the dynamism of his body, calculating his sweeping gestures very carefully, as if he were studying the measured effort of every muscle. Now he has his hands quite flat on the ground, his head close to his knees, concentrating on the effort to fold himself over like a bow that is being bent till the two ends meet. In the East, this is called "Obeisance to the sun". A few seconds pass, and the Yogi stands up again slowly, with no abrupt movements, and his arms describe a large circle before he resumes his starting position.

Bending and stretching, followed by relaxation; relaxation all the more effective because of the expense of effort that preceded it. A sort of current flows rewardingly through the muscles, the nerves and the whole psychical organism. From the body the relaxation passes to the soul, and a feeling of lightness and well-being accompanies it.

The *Deep Obeisance* is an excellent beginning. In Lesson Three, however, I preceded it with an exercise rather different in meaning and effect, since it is an exercise in balancing and not in "dynamism". But the *Tree*, which you already know, brings about, just like the other exercises, that which it represents. In other words, it is one of those freely and purposely performed exercises in which I make my body take up an attitude that corresponds to the attitude I want my soul and spirit to adopt. Let me explain what I mean by this.

Imagine that for some reason or other I am worried. The worry has made me overexcited and nervous. Or you can imagine that I am merely absent-minded; my thoughts are all over the place and my imagination is wandering. As a result I am incapable of work or prayer. But if I manage to take a grip on myself, to do battle with this restlessness, and to stabilize my body by obliging it to maintain a balanced posture for a short while, I am also imposing at the same time a certain immobility on my soul; I am holding it steady and distracting it from all that worries it. I make it pay attention to an action which is apparently alien to it, but which in reality has taken control of it.

My being is well balanced and stable; elevated as well. I am holding myself erect. I have achieved minimal contact (the sole of a single foot) with the ground. My hands are joined together and then stretched up. It is just the same with my soul. Everything in me regroups, everything reaches upwards.

Let me take another exercise still unknown to you: the *Pole*. It consists of standing on your head, resting on your forehead and forearms, with your legs stretched out in continuation of your trunk. Of all the Yogi exercises, this is the most impressive; it is also the one that demands the greatest application and perseverance if it is to be done correctly. It calls for character and energy, since you have to conquer yourself and your apprehensions in order to succeed. It is, therefore, eminently character-building. But that is not all. As well as resting the heart, whose efforts are thus greatly reduced (the blood goes back to the heart by the mere force of gravity), and putting an end to fatigue by irrigating the brain, it liberates a man from two apparently opposite complexes. It gradually eliminates the feeling of fear and gives a man perfect consciousness of balance. With your feet in the air, your motionless body stretched out straight but not tensed (it is, in fact, relaxed, and this upside-down position is the most restful of all), you really feel yourself, you feel that you are in possession, in control, of yourself. A sense of tranquillity flows through you. For the timid and the inhibited this is the end of the painful "inferiority complex". But for the proud, and people who are too sure of themselves, it incites humility. To stand on your head you have to overcome the sensation of doing something laughable. So humble a posture promotes humility. It lifts a man up to heaven, but in a fashion that is the opposite of any haughty attitude. Like the *Tree* posture, it is a "sign" and brings about what it signifies.

The *Deep Obeisance*, the *Tree*, the *Pole* are the three postures which ensure for the Yogi a reward more precious, if possible, than the physical balance I dealt with in the previous lesson; calm, peace and equanimity; a certain

self-mastery. The *Snake*, the *Bent Bow*, the *Plough* and the
Backstretch also have a calming effect by causing certain
factors making for irritability, nervous tension, etc., to
disappear. This is quite a negative effect. The Yogi knows
something better: *Shanti*, something very complex, made
up of balance, confidence in oneself, tranquil assurance,
strength, or rather energy, and true tranquillity.

Think of all these effects when you carry out your
exercises. They will all come in their own time, slowly but
surely. Be sensible; patience must never be lost. But understand clearly what is going on in you, so that you are in a
position to take advantage of it. Tell yourself this very
clearly: during the exercises your soul is cut off from the
outside world and cut off from itself (memories, cares and
worries) and cannot but benefit to the full from a whole
series of phenomena that become evident in the body: the
improvement in the circulation of the blood, the relief of
congestion in certain organs, the stimulation or relaxation
of nerves and muscles, the tonic effect on the brain, the
clearing of the respiratory tracts, the cleansing of the lungs,
the peace of mind, the stimulation of the internal secreting
glands, and so on. These phenomena make their appearance
in the body, but they affect the soul and act on the soul.
They are factors of physiological life; they are equally
factors of the life of the soul (rational and spiritual life).
Peace, the great calm, the *Shanti* of the Yogi, is only the
repercussion on man's inner life of practices in which soul
and body work together in unity, with each other, for each
other and in each other. To this union (Yoga, as I have
said, means "joining together") of the very different
elements in the human complex, the full development,

unconscious, but all the more certain, of what is truly human in each of us, responds.

And now, to work!

PRACTICE

A. RESPIRATION

Exercise 20: Alternate breathing

This consists of breathing in and out alternately through one nostril at a time. The ideal position for it is the *Perfect Posture*, which is not yet familiar to you. So do this exercise standing up, kneeling down or lying on your back.

Place the index finger and middle finger of your right hand on the bridge of the nose. With your thumb, stop up the *right* nostril, then breathe in through the *left* nostril only, counting to 4, 5 or 6 (according to the rhythm you adopt). As soon as you have done this, release the right nostril and breathe out through *both* nostrils, keeping to the same rhythm. Then stop up the *left* nostril with the third finger and little finger and breathe in through the *right* nostril, still keeping the same rhythm 4, 5 or 6.

Repeat: left nostril (breathe in); both nostrils (breathe out); right nostril (breathe in); both nostrils (breathe out).

Do this five or six times running. You can give more time to breathing out (through both nostrils) if you like.

The Indians assure us – and science has confirmed their assertions – that the vital energy (they call it *prāna*) which penetrates us with the air we breathe is polarized, like an electric current. There is a negative *prāna*, absorbed into the organism only through the left nostril and a positive *prāna* which enters only through the right nostril. Alternate breathing, the principle of *prānāyāma* which we shall deal with later, is an application of this theory.

B. POSTURES

Begin by combining, in the way I have taught you, the postures in the previous lesson: the *Tree*, the *Deep Obeisance*, the *Snake* and the *Dolphin*. But between the last two, interpolate the posture known as the *Bent Bow*.

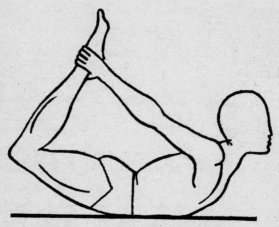

Fig. 18. "THE BENT BOW" (Phase One)

Exercise 21: The Bent Bow

Three times you have raised yourself up on your out-stretched arms (the *Snake*); three times you breathed in deeply as you got up and breathed out deeply again as you returned to your starting position; three times you have turned the hinges of your dorsal vertebrae; and finally you have stretched your stomach (muscles and internal organs) three times. And now you are resting with your face on the floor, fully relaxed, breathing freely, with a pause between breathing out and breathing in.

Now double up your legs to meet your thighs. Reach backwards so as to grasp firmly first one ankle and then the other. Keep your knees slightly apart and exert a strong pull on your arms with your legs (fig. 18).

Your stomach remains firmly on the ground, but your chest is more or less raised according to the strength of the pull you are exerting with your legs. Get your head back as far as you can. Your body forms a sort of bent bow and your arms and legs represent the bowstring. Try to stay like that for a few seconds without breathing; then release the legs, one at a time, and return to the starting position. Do this once only.

To do this exercise perfectly you would have to keep your legs vertical or nearly vertical (fig. 19), and the effort would have to come from the dorsal vertebrae (as in the *Snake*, Second Phase), helped only by the pull of the legs

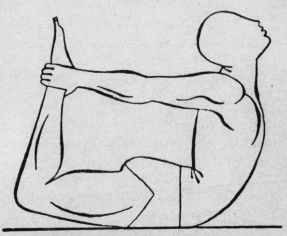

Fig. 19. "THE BENT BOW" (Phase Two)

on the arms. But that is quite a performance. Still, it is as well to have the correct way of doing the exercise in mind right from the beginning.

The effects of the *Bent Bow* are the same as those of the *Snake*, only more pronounced. The posture calls, therefore, for the same reservations in the case of people suffering from spinal or kidney trouble. It can cause an erection – a tiny inconvenience which generally soon disappears – or even urination. Don't stay in the position unnecessarily long. Cut it out altogether if any difficulty arises.

Exercise 22: The Dolphin

After these two exercises (the *Snake* and the *Bent Bow*) which call for exertion, the *Dolphin* (Exercise 4, p. 25) comes as a relaxation. This complements the periods of relaxation (flat on your face with your arms out in front of you) you have already had between each exercise.

If you are not too tired, do the *Half Backwards Bend* (Exercise 11, p. 42) and then the *Backstretch* (Exercise 18, p. 56), followed by the *Pubic Stretch*.

Exercise 23: The Pubic Stretch

Sit down with your legs stretched out in front of you. Fold your legs, keeping the thighs wide apart, and bring the feet together, *sole to sole*. Then pass your arms under the inside of your thighs, with the hands under the legs, and grip your ankles on each side (fig. 20).

Bend the trunk forward and let the head drop as if to touch your heels with your forehead (fig. 21). It will be a long time before you are successful, but you should persevere until one day you master this exercise.

It is really essential to move your feet to the front, to

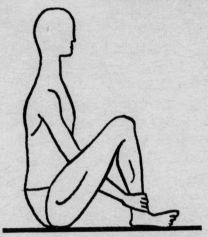

Fig. 20. "THE PUBIC STRETCH" (Phase One)

increase the distance between your thighs and to get your knees closer to the ground. Your elbows should touch the ground and your forearms should be quite flat along your legs. If necessary, push your legs forward a bit (this brings them slightly apart and the soles are turned slightly upwards). And there you are! Well, almost!

But what a strain on the private parts! After a few weeks things will improve, and you will, I am sure, have a weak-

Fig. 21. "THE PUBIC STRETCH" (Phase Two)

ness for this exercise, which combines the *Backstretch* (to be more precise, the vertebral stretch) with the *Pubic Stretch*.

When you first do it, the *Pubic Stretch* sometimes excites the sexual glands. I want to warn you about this. Celibates must not abuse it.

Fig. 22. "RELAXATION"

Exercise 24: The Posture of Relaxation

After so much bending and stretching the exercise called *Relaxation* (fig. 22) comes just at the right time. It looks simple. It is one of the most difficult.

To relax properly is quite an art. We are all "tensed up", perpetually stretched out. Even when we are "stretched out" on our beds, or in an armchair, when we are resting, we are not relaxed, not fully and consciously relaxed. This is all the more true of our working hours. We assume an air of gaiety or sadness, we look busy, preoccupied or even detached, according to the work we are engrossed in. If we are engaged in writing, the attention our mind gives to it is expressed by the tension in our face. We are seldom "natural". Try to stretch out your hand in front of you, but in such a way that it is, as it were, left to itself. Let it hang at the end of your wrist, really hang, and then let the fingers try to take up any position they like. You will manage to get some kind of result, perhaps, after several attempts: you will get pins and needles in your fingers; you will find it hard to keep them still; they will move without any action on your part; but your hand will be relaxed. Any one who took hold of it would certainly be aware of that.

From time to time, you should be able to relax, not only your hand or your face, but your whole body. Here is one way, one exercise among many others, one of the most difficult, as I told you.

Lie down flat on a rug on the ground (your bed is not suitable for this exercise); feet together, or a little at right angles; arms at rest alongside the body; palms on the ground (or, if you like, turned upwards: choose the best position when you have had some experience). There must be nothing pressing against the waist.

Then you will have to "give orders" to your muscles. Starting with your head, go through all the main muscles in your body one after another. Concentrate on each muscle and say, under your breath or even out loud: "Relax; let go; more, more still. . . ." Speak to your muscles as you are *breathing out*, or at the moment you stop breathing and your lungs are empty. When you get as far as the feet, go back to the head and start again. Do that twice; three times if necessary. Gradually relaxation will set in without your having to give orders. You will hardly have taken up your position when you feel yourself go. . . . The Indian Yogis say the body must be "like a bundle of damp linen".

Obviously this means complete immobility. Let your mouth fall open and your lower jaw hang slack. Never mind if you look a fool. Try to lift your arms: they should fall heavily back again; it is a sign of real relaxation.

It is possible that once you are lying down you may feel your heart beating more strongly than usual. Let it beat. Listen to it. It will soon calm down again. Or you may feel the throbbing of the arteries in the temples "as if you had migraine . . .".

The exercise can take a good ten minutes. Complete relaxation takes a pretty long time, especially at the beginning. You can relax like this every night before you go to sleep.

Lesson Five

WHAT DOES HATHA-YOGA LEAD TO?

THEORY

TOWARDS DEVELOPMENT ON THE NATURAL PLANE

I RECENTLY asked you an almost indiscreet question: Are you a man? Are you virile in your actions?

Today I am going further: Are you a Christian? Not just baptized, not just a believer, but a constant witness to the true Christian life?

I am no more pretending to give you a more or less exhaustive definition of man than I was in Lesson Three, and I have no intention at this stage of giving you a description of a Christian, still less of the Christian life. I simply want to tell you the way, one of the ways, I, as a Yogi, like to envisage the disciple of Christ and, to a certain extent, Christian life itself.

You know from the catechism that, at the moment of baptism, supernatural virtue is grafted on to our human nature; a power, a supernatural energy, comes to inform, as it were, the power and energy that make us what we are. This calls for some explanation.

God, by creating me in his own image, gave me something of his own creative power. And I felt it rising within me at the age of puberty; and now, at the height of my

73

manhood, I feel this great desire to produce throbbing
within me, this instinct for paternity which makes me not
want to pass through this world without leaving something
of myself: children, if I am married; other children, other
extensions of myself, if I live in continence; a whole body
of people to show that I have collaborated in the work of
the Almighty.

God gave me this great desire to know, attain, and above
all to embrace, truth, in its entirety, the truth which, from
the days of my childhood, brought so many questions to
my lips that sometimes remained unanswered. I felt my
intelligence expand and grow to welcome a whole world of
realities for which it seemed to be made. I directed my
research and extended my learning far beyond the limits
of what is perceptible and sensible. Finally I found God,
the Truth, which explains and contains the truths I had
encountered during the course of my pilgrimage. But in
finding, I learned that I possessed nothing, or only very
little. Every day I perceive that my desire to know, to
apprehend, is expanding to embrace infinite Truth, the
Word that comprises everything in the bosom of the
mystery of God.

God gave me love – and I do not write that burning
word without infinite reverence – that mysterious dynamism without which my creative energy, my impulse to
learn, would, in the long run, remain sterile; that great
need to commit myself, my whole being, all my knowledge,
to someone, something that I can mould in my own image;
that instinctive consciousness that "alone I am nothing",
alone I can do nothing; but that by giving myself to another,
above all by surrendering to The Other, I find self-fulfilment
as I produce, procreate, invent; love which never tires, love

which surpasses all things, sacrifices all things when it is inspired by him who placed it in me.

Masculine strength, abundant energy; receptive and creative intelligence; love – life, all this God gave me when he made me man; when, as the Bible tells us, he created me "in his own image". And all these things ought freely to increase and grow to the point of making my feeble self a replica, a likeness, distant, but real, of him who created me. Freely? Alas! Something, some sort of catastrophe (faith teaches it, but experience confirms it), clipped the wings, so to speak, right at the outset, of the conscious dynamism of my wonderful human energy. Other powers came to birth in me, hideous caricatures of my virile energies. Their names are "concupiscence", "pride", "ambition" and "lust". They are a sort of disease that has established itself on each plane of my life as a man, in the body of my flesh, in my intelligent soul, in my loving heart.

The gift of God, or *creative Grace*, as the Fathers called it, made me into that masterpiece, that balanced mixture of beauty, power and love that we still admire in Christ, the perfect man, the prototype of all human beings. Original Sin – let me say again that my experience on this subject backs up my faith – brought disorder into this masterpiece. But to sin, the disease that preyed upon humanity, God has provided the remedy. I cannot here in this mere summary of the ideas of the catechism enumerate all the aspects of this new gift of God, which is what *redemptive Grace* is. To enumerate them would be out of the question – they are innumerable – nor could I set out in order the various aspects of the Redemption. I will just pick out one of them: God, by bringing about, through Christ, that recasting, that re-creation, which the priest speaks of in the offertory of the Mass (*et mirabilius reformasti*), did not destroy the nature of those gifts, those powers which, at the beginning of the lesson, we were admiring in man. *Non minuit, sed sacravit.* He did not diminish that nature; he consecrated it. And so we find all its benefits again in Christ: all its benefits, all its powers, intact, but enriched by a new dynamism, made sacred and, as it were, clothed in a divine environment in Christ, in the Christian. . . .

The Christian, what a whole world he is! But without trying to embrace everything in one pale definition, you can say that, *among other things*, he is a *man* whose virile energies are reinforced and consecrated by a power that elevates them and gives them a chance to work, to operate in a divine environment: the very environment that saw the birth and development of the virtues of that perfect man, Christ our Saviour. But let us return to Yoga!

This way of looking at things, putting the accent on one of the well-defined aspects of the work of Creation and Redemption, is familiar to the Christian Yogi, more familiar than to the ordinary Christian. For hundreds of years, as we know, Christian spirituality has mainly tended towards *spiritualism*. Influenced by the dualism of Plato, and more particularly of Descartes, which contrasted body and soul, rather like two antagonists, and located perfection only in the rational element, it scarcely made allowance for any "touching up" on the part of God, for the action of Grace (both creative and redemptive), except on the level of the human spirit, the free and intelligent soul. A perfect Christian is above all a "spiritual" man, a man who lives "according to the spirit". "Spiritualization", says Dr Goldbrunner in this connection, "is the aim of all religious striving. War is declared on the body. The dualism is present in all degrees from open hostility to latent suspicion. Asceticism is a constant wrestling with the body, a suppression of all the dangerous forces of nature, a fight against everything that pertains to the senses. Attack is the best form of defence and so the instinctive lower life of the body was resisted with flagellations, fastings and night-watches, for the purpose of making it serviceable and tractable."[1] This is "the fundamental dualism" between body and soul at work in the practice of and search for sanctity.

The Yogi, the Christian Yogi, rejects this dualism. To this conception of man, a Christian one it may be, but springing from a Christian philosophy cut off from its sources, he prefers, and very much prefers, the ancient, traditional and biblical method of distinguishing three levels in man, three powers: that which presides over the life of the body (*anima*), that which controls the rational life (*animus*), and that which resides in the heart (*spiritus*).[2]

The Yogi seeks perfection in the balanced interplay in him of these three powers, an activity on which the harmony of his being, the development of his personality and the elevation of his inner life depend. He likes to think of divine grace as informing his energies and transposing their activity on a higher, supernatural and divine plane. He does everything he can to dispose his faculties, body, soul and spirit, so that a power coming from on high can take possession of them. In a word, he aspires to develop *on the natural plane* and to be a Christian on all the levels of his being.

He wants to be sound and healthy in body. Not that he is

[1] Josef Goldbrunner, *Holiness is Wholeness* (London, 1955), p. 5.
[2] See *Christian Yoga*, Part II, chapter 1 "An ancient view of man" (London and New York, 1960), pp. 63–79.

trying to escape the ailments and sufferings it may please God to send him, but that he knows that man is diminished by ill-health. Not only does it prevent his attending normally to activities which in fact continue the work of God upon earth – especially once it is permanently established – but it dulls his highest faculties, and there is a danger that his spiritual life, his life of love, may dry up.

He wants to be well balanced, even tempered. He wants to be free. And all the exercises Yoga provides, from body postures and breath-control, which I have already spoken of, to the practice of attention and the liberation of certain powers of the subconscious by concentration, of which I shall speak later, have in fact only one purpose: to make nature sound and healthy, to bring the best out of nature, and to ensure, by doing so, the engagement of the whole man in the duties of his individual life.

To read certain expositions of Yogi disciplines, you can easily get the impression that Yoga separates men from the world, that it means abstraction from the world, not to say, dismissal of the world. Does not the Yogi novice who enters the room where a rug, kept for exercises and meditation, is waiting for him leave the world at the door with his clothes, his daily cares and all his worries? Is he not escaping for a moment, an hour, hours perhaps, from the obligations of real life to be caught up, in a sort of ecstasy, in something indefinite which is called the Absolute, Brahma, the Self? What then? Will he have the courage, when shortly afterwards he puts his clothes on again, to shoulder his humdrum daily tasks once more?

The fears expressed, in good faith, by theorists firmly wedged in their desks are not without foundation. I shall make them my own, to some extent, in the next lesson.

For the moment I shall content myself by bringing against them evidence given spontaneously by Yogi novices who have culled the fruits, equally spontaneous, of a system of Yoga they took up judiciously.

"I first read *Christian Yoga* with suspicion," writes an Englishwoman who goes out to work, "and in the end I threw the book to the back of a cupboard. Some months later, I took it up again, and read it once more, reflecting on it a good deal. After a week, I made a firm resolve to start on some of the exercises, morning and evening, in a spirit of prayer. Perseverance was needed, since I am no longer young and have not got a strong will. That lasted two years. Today I am writing to thank you. Your book has been the instrument of God. Yoga has brought me nearer to him. It makes me live my days in his presence. I go about my duties, whatever they are, in contentment. I no longer get discouraged, not even by certain faults of mine or my impatience. I show my humiliation to the Lord and abandon myself to him. The renunciation he asks of me I have come to accept."

"The discovery of Christian Yoga," observes an African missionary, "is no ordinary event; it is a grace, especially for us. With its help I have discovered a greater facility for intellectual work and meditation than I have ever known before. I also manage to concentrate my wayward and lively imagination. I find it easier to be more open and expansive, to live in a state of general contentment and real and lasting euphoria. Spiritual life has become more attractive to me. I am better fitted for the service of God, and I demand more from myself. A year of experience! I can report that there has been quite a change in my temperament and the amount of work I get through has considerably increased. The time I give up to the exercises is more than balanced by the definitely better quality of the work I do."

Another echo from a Belgian layman: "Your book is much too spiritual for a man of the world. You have reached the heights of Yoga. But you are a religious, belonging to a contemplative order.[1] Now I am a man of the world, a married man and the father of three children. I do not live in an atmosphere of peace and calm; my life is a hectic life, and you have to struggle, so to speak, to live. What then? Without aiming as high as you, I look to Yoga for a healthy body to serve God and man. Health is undoubtedly an important matter, and we ought to do everything we can to gain it and keep it. So let us take up Yoga! Let us control our *animus* by our *spiritus* and spiritualize our bodies. . . ."

This man of the world is right. Yoga, which helps the priest and the missionary to serve God in prayer and ministry; Yoga, which makes it easier for a working woman to carry out her daily tasks and accept the will of God; Yoga, which transforms the temperament of a student and increases his capacity for study, can also help a hardworking family man to do his job well and bring up his children. It should in any case be the characteristic of a Christian Yoga that it can adapt itself to the individual life of each of us; and that because its task is not to diminish nature, or restrain its activities or suppress its legitimate tendencies in any way, but, on the contrary, to bring out the best in it. To make it flourish, not in an artificial, even unreal, environment, but in the circumstances of real life for which it was made and, let me say it once again, on all planes of human existence.

[1] But a missionary, as well!

PRACTICE

A. RESPIRATION

Exercise 25: Prānāyāma

Go back to Exercise 20. Do it ten times, but towards the end, instead of releasing the *left* nostril so as to breathe out through *both* nostrils, stop up the *right* nostril as well, and stay in that position while you count up to 6. The exercise goes like this:

Breathe in (right nostril), count 6;
Hold your breath (both nostrils closed), count 6;
Breathe out (through the left nostril only), count 6.
Then immediately:
Breathe in (left nostril), count 6;
Hold your breath (both nostrils closed), count 6;
Breathe out (right nostril), count 6.

Repeat this double exercise, which is called *prānāyāma* (holding the *prānā*). It seems complicated. It is very simple, once you've got the hang of it: breathe in through one nostril – hold your breath – breathe out through the other nostril – breathe in again through the same nostril, and so on. Stop the minute you feel the least fatigue.

Fig. 23. "THE CANDLE" (Phase One)

B. POSTURES

Combined Exercises 26 and 27: The Candle and the Plough

First go smoothly through the *Tree*, the *Deep Obeisance*, the *Bent Bow*, the *Snake*, the *Dolphin*, the *Backwards Bend* and the *Folded Leaf* postures without a break. Then lie down in the *Relaxation* position.

Bend your legs so that your knees are above your chest (fig. 23). Press on both hands, straighten the legs and raise them to the vertical position. At the same time raise the front of the body in such a way that it follows the movement of the legs and forms a right angle with the head. The neck is bent till the chin touches the chest. Lift up your

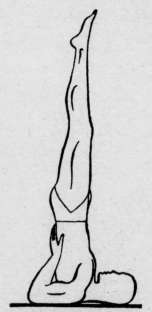

Fig. 24. "THE CANDLE" (Phase Two)

forearms to support the body, holding your hands near your shoulder-blades and supporting them on your elbows. The difficulty arises from the stiffness of the vertebrae of the neck. You will find it very difficult to get your trunk at right angles to your head; your legs have a tendency to curve back in order to keep their balance. But you can only do the exercise correctly by keeping them in a vertical position, as shown in figure 24.

It may help you to do it this way: first, take up the position of the *Half-Candle*, described in Exercise 19 (fig. 17), and then try to bring your legs up to the vertical position in such a way that the feet are over the pit of the stomach (fig. 25). Gradually, as your vertebrae become more

Fig. 25. "THE CANDLE" (Beginner's Stance)

supple, you will be able to push up your seat and slide your hands up to the shoulder-blades, and one day you will achieve the position in figure 24 to perfection. Do not be surprised if this takes a month, two months or more. Meanwhile, thanks to the easier *Half-Candle*, you will not lose any of the benefits of the posture.

Fig. 26. "THE CANDLE" (Intermediate Posture)

Even when you have reached the stage of suppleness, you cannot hold the pose more than a second or two. Then pass to the exercise called the *Plough*, shown in figure 27.

Keep your legs quite stiff and bring them over your head towards the ground. In time they will touch the ground simply by the force of gravity. The hands leave the shoulder-blades and the arms take up a position in continuation of the line of the head. The further the toes are from the head, the more correct the position. But to do this, you need a lot of suppleness in the vertebrae of the neck and a lot of good will.

Fig. 27. "THE PLOUGH"

One variation consists of placing the arms as in figure 28, with the toes coming to rest on the tips of the fingers. Notice the inclined position of the chest, which gives more play to the vertebrae.

So we have two *Candles* (figs. 24 and 25) and two *Ploughs* (figs. 27 and 28). Once you have mastered these exercises, do first the *Candle* (holding the position very briefly), then,

Fig. 28. "THE PLOUGH" (Variant One)

immediately afterwards, the *Plough* (holding the position for some time) and then the *Candle* again (also holding the position for some time). End by taking up the *Posture of Balance* illustrated in figure 29. Arms at the back, hands turned round. You will have to feel your way for some time, but it is an excellent posture for relaxation.

Fig. 29. "THE POSTURE OF BALANCE"

You breathe deeply, but normally, while carrying out these exercises. There is no holding the breath.

During the *Candle*, as in the *Half-Candle*, your attention is fixed on the movement of the blood or on the pit of the stomach; during the *Plough*, on the thyroid gland.

Therapeutic effects. They are undoubtedly considerable. The *Candle* rests the heart – that is its chief merit – and, like the *Plough*, which follows it, it promotes the irrigation of the thyroid. It relieves congestion in the lower part of the abdomen and causes a beneficial massage of the intestines. The *Plough* is recommended for constipation, and also as a discreet bridle for sexual appetites (although, at the outset, it can be the cause of an erection, or even a loss of seed). The two exercises are recommended for the night-time (for once you can do them on your bed, if it is not too soft), since they are an admirable preparation for sleep.

Contra-indications. The *Half-Candle*, the *Candle* and, above all, the *Plough* should be taken up cautiously at first by people who suffer from spinal trouble. The *Backwards Bend* postures can be dangerous if the vertebrae of the neck are not in place. Affections of the other vertebrae (especially the lumbar vertebrae) present less danger.

Lesson Six

WHAT DOES HATHA-YOGA LEAD TO?

THEORY

TOWARDS CHRISTIAN COMMITMENT

IT must be understood that Yoga – through the postures and especially the breathing exercises – automatically releases *great energy*. And I am going to surprise you by telling you emphatically that this is where its danger lies. In fact, if this energy does not find an ouflet, or, to be more precise, if it is not expended to promote the development of the highest faculties of the psyche and the spirit, there is a risk that it may become an obstacle, a factor making for lack of balance; or that, by making the Yogi retire within himself, it may create or bring out in him unfortunate complexes. Think of perfect chastity or perpetual virginity. These virtues have something more than a purely negative aspect. They liberate in those who practise them great powers, which must somewhere find some sort of employment, some opportunity for use, on the spiritual plane (as in the case of monks) or the plane of charity (as in the case of priests and active religious). If they are not controlled and properly directed, there is a danger that these powers may cause disturbance in the inner life of the chaste man or virgin or throw it out of gear. The same danger lies in wait for the Yogi who takes up Yoga without the intention of elevating his life or striving beyond material things towards spiritual and religious realities.

We must reverse the axiom: "He who wills the end, wills the means" and express it thus: "The man who wills the means wills the end". To cut Yoga off from its spiritual purpose is to deny its origins (which, as we have seen, were religious); above all, it is to run the risk, the grave risk, of turning against ourselves the energies it cannot fail to liberate. Not that there is any need for every adept to aim at the mystical, at the summits of contemplation. It is enough for him to have the intention of committing himself in his everyday life to the more generous and more virile practice of his duties as a man, and, what is more, as a Christian.

As a Christian ... that seems simple enough. Yoga, merely by the exercise of quite natural phenomena, surrounds its adepts with an atmosphere singularly favourable to the practice of the evangelical virtues. It calms the senses, appeases the passions and softens manners, while at the same time it is a factor making for serenity, contentment and self-mastery; and it is a duly verified fact that it tends to patience, gentleness and respect for others. Is there so wide a gap between this frame of mind and the ideals of the Beatitudes? No, certainly not! All the more reason for bridging it!

I have by me *Yoga for Everyman* by Desmond Dunne (London, 1951); *Yoga pour soi* and *Yoga pour elle* by Édouard Longue (Paris, 1960); *For Ever Young, for Ever Healthy* by Indra Devi (London, 1955). Excellent handbooks, but they have a serious fault: that pragmatic philosophy that proclaims its aim as the perfection of man by the action of purely natural forces. Subtitles like these: *Live better, live longer*; *For health, charm and happiness*; and *Deliver yourself from evil* are clear enough evidence of the human, almost pagan, tendency of the methods suggested. Other books come under the heading of a dubious esotericism.

The results? A mirage! Twentieth-century man, harassed by the hectic pace of life today, seeks from Yoga, often, too often, an escape from reality. He wants the different postures to provide him with a few moments of peace in which he can find himself again as he really is, without being subjected to all the different pressures of publicity, ideology and the like that his work imposes on him. And so his daily half-hour of Yoga is no more than a parenthesis in the usual run of his daily work. There follows in many cases a sort of painful effort which leads to trouble, first in escaping from reality and then, when he has managed to isolate himself from the world around him, in taking his place again in ordinary life.

Some look for more: they expect to attain, under the unreliable guidance of manuals of an esoteric tendency, those extraordinary powers with which the Yogis of India are credited.[1] They too find Yoga disappointing, because they do not find in it that magical transformation they expected from the mere application of rules of breathing or extraordinary postures.

It is quite certain that all these adepts – there are, alas, some Christians among them – are on the wrong road and are in danger of being lost. For disciples of Christ who want to take up Yoga, the only way out lies in the direction of evangelical perfection. "I do not practise Yoga as an amateur," writes a young African, "but as one who is

[1] On this subject, see Notes and Explanations, section 3, p. 163.

really concerned with it. I think of all it can add to my life and all the changes it can bring. I want to acquire the greatest degree of recollection, reflection and self-mastery, and, above all, those qualities I want to have as the foundation of my life:

1. Absolute integrity, sincerity and frankness;
2. Devotion rooted in God and free of any ulterior motive;
3. Great simplicity, in the very spirit of the Gospel;
4. A will of iron;
5. Absolute purity.

That is the reward Yoga offers. That is why I am interested in it."

It is a matter of *orientation*. It is clear that once a man is committed to Yoga, as a form of asceticism in his life, it will make the most diverse "mystical" virtues flourish and develop, according to the man's zeal and vocation. He is, so to speak, at the disposal of a grace which cannot fail to take advantage of the readiness for co-operation created in the soul of the Yogi by his exercises and disciplines.

When Yoga makes all irritability disappear, when it calms impatience and provides against so many psychological blunders which are so often the consequence of overwork or some imbalance in the organism, it establishes in the adept a gentleness, a certain peace, which makes him more receptive, better able to understand and accept that other gentleness and peace which come from Christ. "Blessed are you who are poor. Blessed are the merciful. Blessed are those who hunger and thirst for holiness." Yoga will help you to understand the meaning and, what is more, the practical value of these evangelical themes. If Yoga makes for "contentment", if it leads naturally to looking on the good side of things, if it makes people optimistic, it is still not the same thing as "abandonment" to Providence. But it opens up infinite possibilities on this plane, to the heart already prepared. The Yogi, generous by nature, will be more sensitive to the approaches from on high. Liberated from some of his chains, released from many kinds of servitude, he will be more supple and more disinterested under the influence of the Holy Spirit. Having become more patient and more enduring, he will often hear more clearly the call to penance.

But Yoga can be of service, and even of assistance, to grace in a special way in the field of prayer.

Note, first, that it disposes to liturgical prayer. The Christian Yogi, more aware of the unity of the human make-up, offers up his whole being (body, soul and spirit) in homage to God. He knows and feels the influence of attitudes of the body on the state of his soul. From his experience of silent and solitary prayer he will know better how to take part in the communal prayer of adoration, praise and petition in which the whole body is invited to express itself. Genuflections, prostrations, movements of the whole congregation in church – the practising Catholic who practises Yoga will want these done properly. He will have instinctively the sense of what Péguy calls the "genuflection of a free man properly carried out". He will associate himself more fully with the gestures of the priest at the altar or, if the occasion arises, with the movements of monks in choir. When he is alone, or when on his rug, he will spontaneously take up the same attitudes of body in which the whole soul finds expression.[1]

[1] See Appendix II: *Symbolic postures and personal liturgy.*

"Silence? Perhaps you think of silence as absence of noise, emptiness in the order of sound? Is it not, on the other hand, fullness in the spiritual order?"[1] One Yogi, commenting on these words by Fr Poucel, wrote: "This is what I experienced this very morning, when my very intense meditation passed without a word, without a syllable, without the least interior sound. Yet my soul found expression. Spontaneous gestures, unprepared, expressed and more than expressed the fullness in my soul."

Silence is not prayer; but prayer, especially contemplative prayer, needs silence: in a sense, it *is* silence, silence that comes down from above or, with the help of a calm disposition, from the depths of the human heart. If man can detach himself from the hubbub of human thoughts and the maelstrom of cares and worries inherent in human life; if he can clear his inner life of all the wanton accumulation that his conscious and unconscious activities have left there, then he will experience that "peace which passes all understanding". It is a peace that knows, though it cannot express it verbally, that in him, the God of Abraham, Isaac and Jacob, the Father of our Lord Jesus Christ, we live, move and have our being, and that "we are his children" (Acts 17. 28), that he is All and we are nothing, unless he fills us, unless we abandon ourselves to him. In fact, the grace that dwells in us, that deifies our deepest self, is eloquent and dynamic. If we are pure and detached from really human values, including thought (discursive thought); if we can escape the currents that sweep us on and the ideas that force us to live in a particular environment; if we can isolate

---

[1] Victor Poucel, *Ma Genèse*, Le Puy (1942), p. 78. From his books, especially *Plaidoyer pour le Corps* (Paris, 1937), Fr Victor Poucel, S.J., may be considered as a precursor of Christian Yoga.

ourselves, live by ourselves for a moment, several moments, the profound reality that makes us what we are, as Christians, must surely make its presence felt and lift up its voice within us.

And that is why, although the manifestations of supernatural life, of divine being and activity, in and around us, are not ours to command, certain human means, like the Yoga postures and breath-control exercises, are effective, admittedly in a purely relative degree, in opening up the way to pure prayer, contemplative prayer. They make the place clean for us. They transform our inner life into that wilderness the prophet speaks of ("It is but love's stratagem, thus to lead her out into the wilderness [*solitudinem*]," Osee 2. 14). They plunge the soul into silence, till it hears, cannot help hearing, the murmur of God's voice, and even the heartrending "groans" of nature (Rom. 8. 22) appealing to God. This nature – assumed by Christ, a branch overflowing with the divine sap – flourishes under the influence of Yoga and its exercises, which order, compose and relax it so well that the power from on high circulates more freely in it and the effective presence of the God of Love is, as it were, more potent.

With this lesson my brief examination of the aims of a Christian Yoga comes to an end. I cannot do better than conclude by quoting, once again, the findings of an adept convinced of the value of Yoga disciplines in the service of a pure, complete and integrated Christianity. Fr Lambert, a Carmelite of Bruges, replying to those "who claim that it is impossible to isolate Yoga from its non-Christian (Buddhist, Hindu, etc.) setting", has this, among other things, to say:

Yoga is essentially human, and it exists for man. It has an intrinsic value, in spite of terms, conceptions and procedures that may be erroneous and unworthy.

This "eternal" Yoga (i.e. Yoga purified from all superstition and freed from its esoteric setting) contains, as we now know, elements of great value. But we know also that it has nothing to offer and that its complete and authentic development is unattainable unless it is assimilated and transfigured into Christ and guided and "informed" by eternal Love and Truth. Its exceptional virtues will only flourish by being transported into the atmosphere of the Light and Love revealed by God. . . .

And must not we Christians shoulder the responsibility for the transfiguration of all the cultural values which until now have wandered far from the fold? They have need of the Word of God: they are waiting for it, and it is our mission to carry it to them. But this cannot be done in the reassuring comfort of our studies, while we content ourselves with playing the part of critics or benevolent spectators. It's practising Yogis that Christ needs![1]

---

[1] L. Lambert, O.D.C., "L'Ancien Yoga et l'homme nouveau", in *Rythmes du monde* (1960), vol. VIII, p. 162. It may be appropriate to quote the conclusion of the same article: "I hope it will be clear from what I have said above that Yoga can exert a really spiritualizing influence; it can help man to realize his spiritual dignity, and it offers a technique which helps to achieve what the etymology of the word implies: putting the body under the *yoke* of the spirit and the spirit itself under the same *yoke* as its First Principle. All this would be clearer still if it were possible to demonstrate the numerous concrete applications of Yoga: in hygiene, therapeutics, education, in all kinds of intellectual activity for gaining and safeguarding moral virtues (in women especially), in the life of the priest and the monk. It will be agreed that here we have a remarkable contribution to the real and full development of modern man" (*ibid.*, p. 179).

PRACTICE

A. RESPIRATION

Just repeat the exercise from the previous lesson:

Breathe in (left nostril), count 6.
Hold your breath (both nostrils closed), count 6.
Breathe out (right nostril), count 6.
Breathe in (right nostril), count 6.
Hold your breath (both nostrils closed), count 6.
Breathe out (left nostril), count 6.

And do that ten times. This will be a big step forward to Lesson Eight.

B. POSTURES

Do the *Deep Obeisance* and the *Tree* and combine with them this posture:

Exercise 28: *The Triangle*

Stand upright, with your legs apart. The further apart they are, the more correct the posture will be. Raise the arms to the horizontal position, palms turned upwards. Breathe deeply, two or three times.

Turn the trunk completely to the *right*, so that your arms are in line with your shoulders all the way along and at right angles to the line of your legs. *Breathe in.* Then *breathe out* and at the same time bend the trunk until the fingers of your left hand are touching the toes of the *right* foot. The right arm is still in line with the left. The head is turned slightly upwards (fig. 30).

After a very short time, raise the trunk again, *breathing in* at the same time and keeping the arms stretched out. Take two or three deep breaths, and then turn the trunk to the

Fig. 30. "THE TRIANGLE"

left and bend it (while breathing out) until the fingers of
the *right* hand are touching the toes of the *left* foot. Do this
once. Breathe in as you get up again and let your arms fall
gently to your sides.

Instead of placing your fingers on your toes, you can
practise putting them *on the ground*, right between your legs.
It is a little more difficult.

People suffering from spinal or kidney troubles can do
this exercise provided they go about it cautiously and do
not force themselves to touch their toes or the ground.

The therapeutic effects of this *āsana* are obvious: it activates the muscles of the side and back and makes the spine and pelvis more supple. If you do it when you get out of bed in the morning, as soon as you have washed, it is excellent, as it overcomes the stiffness of the bones and muscles.

Afterwards do the *Snake* (three times), the *Bent Bow* (once) and the *Dolphin*, but include a period of relaxation between the last two postures: lie on your face and stretch your arms; let yourself go; let the whole weight of your body fall on the rug; relax properly. This variant of the posture of relaxation is sometimes more efficacious than the other, especially when it is introduced between the *Bent Bow* and the *Dolphin*.

Exercise 29: The Full Backwards Bend

You start off from the *Dolphin* position. Bend your knees and keep your buttocks back as in Exercise 5. Sit up and sit back *on your heels*, or better still, *between your heels*, with the tips of your toes touching. Stick out your chest and get your shoulders back and let yourself go backwards. You can support yourself with one hand on a piece of furniture, or you can fall on your elbows the first time. The back should curve as much as possible and the head come to rest, upside down, on the ground (you are looking at the wall behind you, from the upside-down position). The arms are thrown back (fig. 31).

Fig. 31. "THE FULL BACKWARDS BEND"

You breathe in before you let yourself go backwards. Once you are in position, you breathe out gently and carry on with your breathing in the usual way. Then you concentrate on the pit of your stomach (the solar plexus, that accumulates energy).

You can also (fig. 32) cross your arms under your shoulder-blades or even let them fall alongside the body, which has the effect of expanding the chest. Some people put them under the neck, like a sort of pillow.

Fig. 32. "THE FULL BACKWARDS BEND" (Variant)

There are three difficulties to be overcome: (1) Hollowing the back: this calls for a lot of suppleness in the spine, but the other exercises have prepared you for that; (2) putting up with the tension on the muscles of the stomach and thighs[1] (it is obvious that people with a delicate *rectus abdominis* must exercise great caution); (3) being able to breathe: at first it takes one's breath away, and one is tempted to give it up as impossible. With time this difficulty, like the others, will disappear.

Stay in position for a few seconds only. Make use of your hands to get up again. Later on, you will manage to get up by the action of your vertebrae alone, just as you will manage to let yourself fall without support.

[1] I advise beginners to keep their knees apart, but they must keep them on the ground.

This is an essential posture. Its action is most efficacious on the internal organs (including the liver) which it stretches; on the rachis (spinal marrow) and the nerve centres, especially the solar plexus (on a level with the pit of the stomach); and on the chest, which it expands as far as possible. You must therefore manage to do it successfully.

After this strenuous exercise, the *Folded Leaf* (Exercise 12) provides a very pleasant means of relaxation. Take your time and breathe deep and long.

You can end with the *Candle*, the *Plough* and finally the *Posture of Relaxation*.

Lesson Seven

THE LIFE OF A YOGI

THEORY

EFFECTIVE PRESENCE

WE have seen what Yoga is and how far it takes its adepts. Now we penetrate into the very life of the Yogi and come to that difficult art, more difficult than the postures, if not than breath-control, which are an introduction and preparation for it: the art of thinking, reflecting, concentrating, and the first step towards it: the art of giving attention, being present in what one is doing.

There is no external sign by which you can recognize a Yogi, especially a Christian Yogi. He is of his environment and in it. On principle he abhors anything that makes him obtrusive. And yet a practised eye can recognize him: by his walk (he tends to walk "like an Indian" from time to time); by his bearing: he stands up straighter and when sitting rarely leans back; above all by his gestures: he puts *himself* into every move he makes; he carries them out better (you can quickly recognize at the altar a priest who practises Yoga).

Yes, a Yogi does better, he makes a conscious effort. He tries to put his whole self into what he does. He avoids routine, automatism. He tries to be deliberate and, as it were, the master of his reflexes. He wants to be self-possessed so that he can really carry out what is asked of him; and to accept whatever comes his way. Habit robs men of much merit. Their actions suffer because the agent is not effectively and efficaciously present in what he does; the man does not actually "live" the work he carries out; his words and actions are not inspired by a true consciousness of what he is saying or doing.

We are too easily distracted from our activities. The intention suffers in consequence and the result lacks effect.

If we are to do better, we must be completely "with it" – to adopt a phrase. What a Yogi wants is to ensure his effective presence in all he does. How often in a day do we actually give ourselves up to what we are doing? Sometimes, we certainly do and the result is good work effectively done. But we have to admit that modern techniques impose on us a rhythm of life which rarely leaves us time to be present – consciously – at what we do, to be, for more than a moment, what we are.

To illustrate this, let me tell you about a day in the life of a man I know well (my brother, an engineer in Paris). He used to get up – or rather he used to spring out of bed – at about twenty to six and rush into the bathroom. Ten minutes later he was ready. Without stopping for breakfast (when he wasn't too late he would swallow a cup of coffee) he would rush to the station, exactly seven minutes away. He had worked out the distance carefully, and if he left the house seven and a half minutes before the train went he was sure not to miss it. Half an hour in a suburban train; a second cup of coffee at the Gare de l'Est, then the Métro and the office; getting through the mail, interviews, estimates and so on. . . . About ten o'clock he allowed himself a short break, a quarter of an hour. Time to rush round to the nearest café and swallow a *croissant* and another cup of coffee. Over lunch he took as little time as possible, and after it he allowed himself a brief rest in his office which subsequently kept him busy until about five. Then it was time to catch the Métro again and the train home. This was the time for reading the newspapers and talking things over with his friends. From the station to the house, the same regulation seven minutes. Dinner in the evening and the midday rest were perhaps the two things my brother did really well, the things he took time over, the things he really enjoyed and during which he seemed relaxed. Even then it only needed the telephone to disturb his lunchtime rest, or the children to be too noisy at night, or his wife to be overburdened with problems, for him to be upset.

How often that overcrowded day gave me the impression of a race; at least of something rushed, empty, exhausting and chaotic. I am sure that if my brother had known about Yoga and had taken the trouble to include in his day the ten minutes or quarter of an hour of exercises that I have suggested (for instance, on returning from the office or even at bedtime), his life would have been transformed. Yes, those ten "wasted" minutes would have taught him, for instance, to take time to get to the station; to turn that rush into a pleasant walk; to see something on the way; to rest his eyes in the evening when he came home – his eyes, his body and his whole mind; finally to distract himself by a thousand and one things that nature and providence have scattered on our path and which we pay no heed to.

It is a fact that the practice of Yoga teaches people to see things calmly; to let one's eyes rest on things, without getting tired; and to let oneself be carried away by their refreshing and consoling charm. To see, or rather to look, you have to be relaxed, and your mind has to be detached; your body must be liberated and "abandoned". Now Yoga makes this liberation, this detachment, this abandonment of our whole being, a reality.

That is, of course, if the adept does exactly what is asked of him: does the exercises properly, controls his breathing carefully; and also if he does some special exercises in *concentration*, or more simply *attention*.

PRACTICE

A. EXERCISES IN ATTENTION

You know already how to be attentive. During the fifteen or twenty minutes you devote to Yoga exercises, particularly the postures, your soul and body are closely linked and working together. You oblige yourself to concentrate exclusively on the movements you are making, so that they are not those of an automaton. You are fully yourself. All routine is avoided. As soon as you have mastered the postures so far outlined, I will teach you how to make them more difficult, so that each movement will require complete concentration.

Equally, the breath-control exercises demand your full attention. Learn to follow your breathing consciously; accompany the air you inhale as it infiltrates into the furthest cranny of your lungs, as it enriches, purifies and drains your blood. "I am breathing: I am being nourished, I am breath-.ing in strength, I am breathing in life! I am breathing: I open my mouth, I breathe your breath, O Lord (says one of the psalms), and afterwards I calmly and quietly expel the impurities of my body." What an excellent exercise in attention, in efficacious concentration!

But now for some more exercises.

Exercise 30: "Placing" your eyes

Choose a familiar and quite quiet spot where you are completely alone; a shady corner, but not too dark. First do the following eye exercises:

Make your eyes swivel to a point on your extreme left; then to a point on your extreme right:

From B, return to A, directing your gaze upwards as you do so; then return to B (by the upper route). From B, direct your gaze towards point C, then D. Go back to A and pass to B, then D, to A, then C. Go back to B and start again.

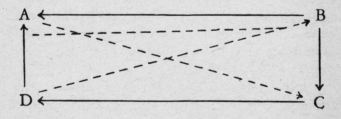

Alternatively: A – B – C – D – A, then A – C – D, then D – B – C, and finally C – B – A – D. Don't tire yourself. When you've finished, close your eyes.

Now open your eyes and try to "place" them; literally place them on the lawn in front of you, on that tree, that clump of flowers. Let your eyes rest there, and let that green carpet, that mass of leaves, those multi-coloured flowers make their impression on you so that you form an impression of them in your mind in the way that a photo-sensitive film would.

You will soon realize how difficult this simple exercise really is. We are too accustomed to see a multitude of things passing before our eyes as in a film without paying more than the vaguest attention to them. Only moving objects make an impression on us and then only because the movement obliges us to notice them; we seldom therefore consciously observe anything. It may be that we were struck by the "line" of that car at the crossroads just now. We thought we saw it for a moment but it disappeared almost instantly. And everything that passes backwards and forwards in front of our eyes during the course of the day is like that car. Cinema ... that is our daily life.

Learn anew how to look, how to see properly, quietly, steadily, calmly, at least some things during the course of your day. Give yourself sufficient time to observe a few things consciously. I do not ask you to stare at, or to analyse, what you see. Later, if it is necessary, you will learn to fix your attention on things so as to make a visual, analytical examination. Today just learn how to enjoy nature and let your subconscious fill up with beautiful images. Make no effort to engrave these impressions on your memory. Allow your eyes to wander where they will. It is sufficient that you have the minimal intention of noticing what you see. You will be surprised, after some weeks of re-education, to see so many things, and to see them so clearly. You will find it restful, just letting your eyes rest on things like that.

Exercise 31: *Listening*

Quietly looking at things is an art. So is listening. But here again the art has been largely lost. The cinema ruins our eyes; the radio and the noise and vibration of town life deleteriously affect our hearing. Rehabilitation in this case is more difficult than in the case of the eyes. Silence, which gives you a chance to hear things, is so rare. Yet there are intervals when everything around us seems to be silent. Let us take the opportunity provided by such intervals to listen for sounds less noisy than those which normally engulf us.

For instance, if you have a garden you could use it in the evening as a place of recollection and quiet. Try to listen for some familiar sound: perhaps there are birds in the neighbourhood; a little stream that flows not far away; even the noises from the nearby town, confused noises, but we can discern certain sounds above and beyond the general racket. Let us listen, open our ears, so that one sound penetrates them, takes refuge there, comes to impress itself on our brain. Do not listen as though you were straining to catch the words of a lecturer up at the other end of a hall. Whatever you do, suppress tension, try to be passive so that you can hear more clearly.

My advice to you is not to analyse. If you play a gramophone record, do not try to identify the tempo and the movements of the particular sonata. The exercises in this lesson are exercises in "intentional passivity" (comparable with the conscious and intentional relaxation of the *Relaxation* posture: the principle is the same). Music, birdsong, the murmur of the stream, the noises of the town must quite simply make their own impression on your ears. You are attentive, but fully relaxed. Listening under these conditions is true repose; it is also a re-education process which will finally enable you to hear more clearly and with greater profit.

Exercise 32: Touching, feeling

This is a matter of developing the senses so as to obtain an exact appreciation, independent of thought, of the outside world. We have to become consciously receptive, with the intention of taking in nothing other than impressions of external origin, and of refusing to be distracted by what comes from within.

Stretch out your hand and touch a table, a chair, a piece of material, and note the first impression this contact creates. Think of nothing but feeling, recognizing, touching. Put your fingers gently on the window and carelessly move them up and down. Then touch your clothes, and then the table and the upholstery. Notice quickly the sensation of cold given by the glass, the soft warmth of the garment, the ridges in the table.

Exercise all your senses in this way: smell (smoke, flowers); learn for a moment how to enjoy them all. Observe them and be alive to them.

Exercise 33: Walking

Nothing is more common. We walk miles in the course of a day. Let us reserve a few moments, five minutes for instance, for a conscious walk. Stand erect with your shoulders back (don't overdo it); let your arms hang down, palms to the front. Walk steadily, keeping in step with your breathing; for instance, four steps as you breathe in, five or six as you breathe out. Oblige yourself to be aware of the motion of walking; for instance, pay attention to the contact of your foot with the ground, whether it is more or less hard; feel your knees bend; listen to the noise you make as you walk. Do all this deliberately, with your eyes fixed steadily on the landscape straight in front of you. You will soon feel all stiffness go from your limbs and all heaviness disappear. You will feel supple, and walking will rest you.

This may seem trivial and childish. Try it. If you pay attention like this when you are out walking, you will be able to adopt a restful walk and go a long way without feeling too tired afterwards. You will also cultivate your awareness and prepare yourself to be the master of your own actions.

Exercise 34: Reading aloud

This is a matter, to be more exact, of being attentive to your reading, *listening to yourself reading*, either aloud or mentally. Take up a text, easy or difficult, it doesn't matter, and read it out loud or in a low voice, without bothering too much to understand what you are reading. What counts in this exercise is that you should *hear* yourself read; that the sound of the letters, the syllables and the words should strike your ears; that you should be fully conscious of the different intonations dictated by the general sense and punctuation. In short, listen to yourself reading as though you were listening to someone else.

You will find it considerably easier to understand a difficult text if you first read it aloud in this way.

By running through the text mentally, by hearing the sound of it in your ears, your subconscious will take a firm impression of it. If you then ignore the text for twenty-four hours, you will find, on taking it up again and reading it

with regard this time to its meaning, that you will understand any difficult passages in it much more quickly.

B. POSTURES

You will find it an advantage to make yourself familiar
with those "squatting" postures so current in the East.
There are several of them, basically variations of the same
initial posture. I told you in Exercise 13 (pp. 44–45) about
an excellent preparation for the posture called the *Perfect
Posture*. This preparation is valid for all the postures we are
going to do. I take it for granted that you have practised it.

Exercise 35: The Perfect Posture
Preparation and Variant One

Material necessary (at first) in addition to the rug or mat
you usually work on: a fairly large pillow, or cushion, and
a rolled-up rug.

Sit down in the centre of the pillow and slip the rug under
your seat. Keep the thighs wide apart.

Bend your left knee and put your left leg in front of you
so that the heel comes right in the middle of the body, under
the sex organs, and the ankle in front of them and slightly
underneath. If you have practised the posture in Exercise 13
on p. 45 (reproduced here in fig. 33) you will have to
modify it a little, keeping the thighs wider apart and bringing the heel more to the right: get it really in the centre
and slip it *slightly* under the perineum.

Then bend the right knee and put the right foot on the
left foot, ankles crossed. The right heel is then also in the
centre (or a little towards the left; it partly covers the sex
organs). The tip of the right foot rests on the left leg or is

Fig. 33. "THE PERFECT POSTURE" (Preparation)

Fig. 34. "THE PERFECT POSTURE" (Variant One)

lightly inserted between the leg and the thigh. The toes of the left foot may stick out under the right leg, in front (fig. 34).

The only difficulty as far as I can see is to keep the thighs as far apart as possible (this may cause some pain afterwards in the private parts, but this pain will go, like the others). The hands are placed as in the illustration. The trunk must be quite straight. If it helps you can rest your spine against a piece of furniture.

Look fixedly in front of you, blinking as little as you can. You can also bend your head and look fixedly at your heel, or even your navel. Absolute immobility is of the greatest importance.

Fig. 35. "THE PERFECT POSTURE" (Variant Two)

Exercise 36: The Perfect Posture

Variant Two

For some people, this posture is easier to take up than Variant One. The right foot (or the left foot) is placed alongside the left leg (or the right) and the heel pushed right into the fold in the groin (the sex organs take their place between the leg and thigh, behind the heel). Lean forward and take hold of your left foot (or your right) with your hand and place it on your right (or left) leg, sole uppermost. Sit up again (fig. 35).

The difficulty here is to keep both knees firmly on the ground. It is not insurmountable. You will find it easier to take up this position if you sit on a pillow and slip a rug under your seat.

Fig. 36. "THE PERFECT POSTURE"

Exercise 37: *The Perfect Posture*

Here now is the *Perfect Posture* proper. You have to slide your left heel right under the perineum, and even under the anus; the sole of your foot is turned uppermost, and the right buttock and thigh rest on it.

Then, as in the preceding exercise, you take the right foot with your hand and place it on your left leg, or to be more precise, insert it between the leg and the left thigh, with the toes pressing on the calf (fig. 36).

Fig. 37. "THE HERO POSTURE"

If you have a rolled-up rug under your seat, it will prevent a certain contortion and make it possible for you to stay astride your heel without too much pain.

Let me say clearly that every success in these exercises represents a victory, and every victory has to be paid for.

The difficulties vary greatly from one person to another. They obviously depend on certain anatomical peculiarities: the length and thickness of the thighs, whether one is fat or thin, and so on. But they depend more on the will and the imagination. Before you go to sleep at night, conjure up the different postures and the method of doing them in your mind's eye.

Exercise 38: *The Hero Posture*

This is a variation of the *Perfect Posture*. Once the right foot is placed along the left leg (or vice versa) the opposite foot is placed, sole uppermost, *on* the thigh, with the heel resting against the abdomen (fig. 37).

The right foot can also be placed *under* the thigh or under the opposite knee. The trunk must be quite straight.

Fig. 38. "THE LOTUS" (Preparation)

A "heroic" posture indeed, which calls for a strong will; but after a period of persevering practice it becomes quite pleasant. At the outset you should maintain the position for a very short time. You will gradually improve and succeed in holding it for longer.

Don't worry if you get a pain in the joints. It will go.

Exercise 39: The Lotus

And now, by way of conclusion, the Yogi posture *par excellence*: the *Lotus*. It is no good starting on this until you have mastered the other postures in this lesson.

Fig. 38 shows the starting position. The left foot is placed firmly on the right thigh, with the heel pushed right into the fold in the groin. The right leg is bent inwards as shown in the illustration.

Fig. 39. "THE LOTUS"

Hold the leg firmly on the thigh with one hand; with the other take hold of the foot resting on the ground by the instep; pull hard till it comes on to the opposite thigh, as near as possible to the groin (fig. 39).

Your legs are literally tied up (and you will have some trouble untying them). The Indian Yogis cross their hands behind their backs and grasp each of their big toes with their fingers. But that is a performance of which few Europeans are capable unless they have long arms.

Exercise 40: Resting

If you are a beginner, I strongly advise you not to maintain any exercise for more than a few moments. You should rest quite frequently. Lean back against the wall (or a piece of furniture) and bring your knees up close to your chin. Keep your feet quite flat on the ground, pressed against each other (with the heels touching the sex organs). Fold your arms around your shins and rest your head on your knees.

You will soon feel the benefit of this squatting position. After a few minutes' relaxation, you will find it easier to take up the *Perfect Posture* again, or its first variant.

I have given you the five essential postures of Yoga in one lesson so that I shall not have to come back to them again. A good Yogi is capable of taking up all five correctly, and this is a sign that he has become, to some extent, the master of his body.

But of course you must not try to do them all at once. The order in which I have given them represents a gradual process of training; but it is quite possible that the *Perfect Posture* will become familiar to you before its first variant.

Anyway, you will have your preferences, and for meditation I would advise you to make a habit of choosing the one you find most agreeable.

It is, in fact, particularly for meditation that these exercises are designed. But not exclusively: they make excellent postures for relaxation. And if you already find them useful for the exercises in attention I gave you at the beginning of this lesson, that would be a great advantage.

Courage! You are of course still practising the exercises you learnt in previous lessons. Soon I shall teach you how to make a selection from these exercises so that you are able to reserve most of the time you have at your disposal for meditation.

Lesson Eight

THE LIFE OF A YOGI

THEORY

CONCENTRATION

You can be a good Yogi without being able to do exercises like the *Candle* or the *Full Backwards Bend*. On the other hand, you cannot cross the threshold of Yoga, true Yoga, until you have learned to fix your mind on an idea, to concentrate, meditate, on something according to well-defined rules. Hence the importance of this lesson, which is devoted to concentrating the mind.

Concentration is the opposite of dissipation. It is the state of a mind whose faculties have, as it were, made a reconnaissance (on the look-out for something to make the object of a thought) and which then attempts to bring these faculties back to base, where there will be only one idea.

In fact, there are two kinds of concentration. In the first, which I shall call *active concentration*, we apply our powers to a single object, a single idea. In the second, *passive concentration*, we are possessed, we are worked on, perhaps unknown to ourselves, by a subject or idea. This brings into play an enormous factor in our human life: the subconscious. To liberate the subconscious, furnishing it with the opportunity and the means to work, is the art of the Yogi.

"Sleep on it", people say. It is true that, during sleep, in which we rest our conscious faculties, our subconscious powers work on the solutions of problems we have been dealing with, apparently in vain, during the day. A forgotten idea, or rather one we have cast aside (because we did not see what it could lead to), can come to life again in our minds, with the help of the night, and reveal its riches, which will sometimes be presented to our minds on waking.

Here is another example: something preoccupies us; we turn the problem over from all angles; we discuss it, we worry about it; all for nothing. Suppose some incident then occurs which *distracts* us. Suddenly, the solution is clear! We try, fruitlessly, to remember a name and when we are no longer thinking about it that name comes to our mind.

Think of the writer who explores an idea and sketches out on paper the thoughts it suggests to him. If he is wise, if he is clever, he will put it by, once he has finished the page and go and do something else. The next day, when he takes up his work again, he will find that, without any great effort, he can improve and perfect it. The greatest discourses have seldom been pronounced as they were written. Between the time when the orator, pen in hand, got his ideas together, and the time when he delivered the discourse, the subconscious had gone to work, and the happiest formulas thus appear to be the most spontaneous.

These examples from everyday life show us that the two kinds of concentration operate together. Active concentration (effort) usually precedes passive concentration (the work of the subconscious). But it can happen the other way about. The main thing is to understand that concentration is not merely a tremendous tension of the mind with a view to suppressing the customary waywardness of our thought processes and so forcing the mind to single out a well-defined subject. An appreciation of the process of concentration should also suggest to us an idea of the confidence we place in our subconscious faculties or the more subtle powers of the human mind.[1]

PRACTICE

A. A METHOD OF CONCENTRATION

1. *Beyond the threshold: relaxation and centralization*

The threshold of concentration, as we saw in Lesson Seven, is the art of paying attention. That art we have practised "passively" – already applying, therefore, one of the great principles of Yogi concentration – by trying to let images, noises and all sorts of sensations take possession of us and make their impression on us. Now we go a step further: we analyse and centralize. A few concrete examples will show us the way.

1. I am sitting down (in the *Perfect Posture*) in a quiet corner of my garden, absolutely alone at a time when everything is calm. I am motionless, and a series of rhythmic breathings or a few *prāṇāyāmas* have brought me calm. I simply let my eyes rest on the familiar landscape (see above, pp. 105–6) and put all reflections away from me. I am bathing in an atmosphere of calm, relaxation and repose, and after a few minutes this leads quite naturally to concentration.

I gradually get my mind off what I can see, and I try to

[1] See my book *Christian Yoga*, pp. 64–79.

pick up a single idea. All around me is calm, silence. Good! I will think of "calm – silence – relaxation – repose". I will repeat these words several times mentally or in a low voice. This will soon establish a connection between my physical state (lively relaxation), my psychical state (without anxiety) and my thought: hence – easy concentration.

In the same atmosphere of conscious relaxation I can also think of "light", "luminosity", "brightness"; and, if need be, I shall conjure up a picture of all the lights I know, all the kinds of light, from the brightness of the stars to the fire of the midday sun. From the thought of "light" I pass to the thought of him who is the "true light", "who enlightens every soul born into the world". I shall repeat these formulas under my breath. I shall see this "Word" that is "Light"; I shall see it in my mind's eye: Christ enlightening the world; Christ bringing light to his contemporaries, to ourselves; the image of Christ, the "light" that "shines in the darkness", will take hold of me. A few minutes like that will be first-class "concentration".

Provided I do not immerse myself in noise again too quickly, my subconscious will pursue the idea – a very important phase in Yogi psychology. And tomorrow, or the day after, in the same spot, in the same atmosphere of calm, I shall concentrate once more, and from the ideas of the day, like the lights of many lamps lit at the same spot, will proceed one single idea, and that idea I shall make the subject of my meditation.

2. In a corner of my room (always the same corner), I am in the *Perfect Posture*. I fix my eyes, without blinking, on an object – an image, a statue, a crucifix. This image I engrave on my heart, or rather I let it engrave itself on me, focus itself within me. I close my eyes and see it again. I form

an intense image of it in my mind. It will be something upon which to centre my concentration.

Suppose it is a crucifix. I concentrate on the idea of "cross" and try to see all that is attached to this idea of "cross": suffering? Yes, but not just any kind of suffering: suffering that is accepted, welcomed, not merely undergone; suffering that elevates, suffering that ennobles.

From the idea of suffering I pass to the idea of "strength", "energy": suffering accepted always implies strength. I think of my own sufferings – certain quite definite things I have suffered – and I think of the strength I displayed or lacked on that occasion. I see how I shall react in future, perhaps tomorrow; I shall display true strength.

You see the way: you begin with an idea to hang things on, and you pass from it and through it to complete commitment of your whole being.

3. I am breathing deeply and concentrating on the air that is entering my lungs. I can see this air I am thirsting for, I can feel it filling up and regenerating my whole being. With my blood, which it purifies in a marvellous two-way action (as the alveoles of my lungs bear witness), it reaches the very depths of my life as a man and a Christian, increases my strength and enlarges my heart. Concentrating on this everyday phenomenon I pass again to the idea of "life", "strength", "energy". It is easy to see how repeated exercises in concentration on the idea of "strength" make us stronger, more energetic, more sure of ourselves (through the action of the subconscious).

4. From time to time, I shall make a sort of examination of conscience, that is to say, I shall mentally parade, before my mind's eye, the day that is past, or some other day particularly full of events in which I was personally engaged.

(What an excellent form of concentration for a monk to re-live the day of his profession; for husband and wife to re-live the day they said "yes". A priest, calling to mind his ordination, will fix his eyes on his hands, which that day received their definitive consecration.) Or else I shall see *tomorrow*, so that its known occupations will pass in procession before me, a series of generous acts into which I shall really put myself. "I will everything that will happen to me," as Dr Vittoz so well says, "in advance."

A few exercises of this kind and life, to my surprise, will get easier. By reviewing mentally, before I go to sleep at night, the different movements that go to make up the proper way of doing an exercise, I make that exercise easier to do next day; and in the same way, by committing myself to a foreseen – or even unforeseen – future, I am preparing myself to face up to all the circumstances and react calmly to them.

We can see that true concentration, first active, then passive, is not just an intellectual operation; it is not merely the "centralization" of a mind thinking around an idea: it is the bringing together of all the powers of man: the union, the joining, within him, of *anima*, *animus* and *spiritus*, with a view to conscious activity.

2. *The heart of Yoga: visualization, localization, identification*

Beyond the stage of simple concentration, active or passive, there are other disciplines, or more properly, other states, known to Indian Yoga, which are so many steps towards a phenomenon, ecstatic in nature, called *samaadhi* (or *samâdhi*), in which the Yogi identifies himself with the object of his contemplation, with God himself.

Although contemplation, at the heart of Christian life, is

in its essence and nature different from *samâdhi*, the Christian, the Christian Yogi, is by no means forbidden to prepare himself for and dispose himself to contemplation by methods inspired by those which lead to *samâdhi*. In the course of Lesson Six (above, pp. 92-3) I sketched out a sort of metaphysical psychology of pure prayer, contemplative prayer, and likened it to silence, a sort of unfathomable silence that takes hold of the human soul. This "silence" – pure passivity – it is not in the power of man to create or produce, as mystics of all the ages have said again and again in a thousand different ways. They have nevertheless recommended methods of prayer and ascetical exercises designed to make it easier for this type of "silence" to take possession of the human soul. Hence the disciplines – Yogi in form but Christian in spirit – described here.

I am going to repeat the exercises given above, but this time giving them a more spiritual emphasis.

1. Instead of forming a picture of light, the light all around me, for instance, and proceeding from there to the source of all light, I *visualize* a particular light. I light a candle and look steadily at the flame, breathing calmly and deeply in the rhythm I have made my own. After looking at it a minute or two without blinking, I close my eyes and try to go on seeing the flame with my inward eye. After a certain time, and after I have done a certain number of exercises, each time focusing on the same flame with my eyes open, then imagining, visualizing it with my eyes closed, I must get to the stage where I somehow possess that form of light. I must be able to see it, not outside myself, but inside: not external to myself, but living and burning within me. For instance, I locate it, localize it, in my heart, and I see it shining and lighting up all the recesses

of this heart of mine, rich in lofty thoughts, or warming and reviving my generous affections and impulses. I shall end up by *identifying* that flame with my heart, seeing the latter as a fire burning with love, energy consuming itself, not for itself but for others, a fire first lighted, then made to burn brighter, by another power, a power coming from on high.

The three phases of this exercise (I shall find it difficult at first to stick to one of them) have taken me how long? Ten minutes, a quarter of an hour, at the most! There is no point in exceeding this time, and in any case it's impossible. Ten minutes! That, you will say, is too little. It does not give me time to concentrate. All right! But ten minutes today, ten minutes tomorrow and the next day and the days after that, ten minutes of concentration on the same object, that is a lot; it is enough, at any rate, for the result we are aiming at, and that I shall speak of in a moment.

2. When I have exhausted, so to speak, in part, in very small part, the symbolism of the flame, the image of the Cross will become the object of my concentration. I shall localize it on my breast, on my forehead or in my heart; and I shall try to identify myself with him who found on it, and in it, the expression of the greatest love the world has ever known.

3. All noble objects evoke in our eyes some profound reality of an ontological, metaphysical or spiritual kind. As such, when properly seen, properly looked at, *visualized*, they lend themselves to *localization*, in my inner self, and then to *integration*, *identification* with some part of myself or the whole of myself. A translucent glass, an alabaster vase full of perfume, a flower in full bloom, a leaf carried by the wind, can also serve as something on which to

hang fruitful, formative and above all elevating meditations.

Take this flower, this flower floating on the still waters. It draws its sustenance from their depths; but it has been made so that it opens in the daytime and drinks in the sunlight the whole day long. Hardly has the sun disappeared when it contracts naturally and closes its petals. All day long it has been drinking and breathing in light and heat (that is why it is so beautiful). But how sad it is now, in the evening, how withdrawn into itself in a gesture of humiliation and fear. Tomorrow I shall find it full of joy, open again, cup full and running over. This flower is only a flower, only beautiful, when it is in communion with the light of the sun from on high.

I am that flower. The life in me, my human strength, is like that flower; it is that flower. Its roots, I know them well! And I know, too, the different levels of my being at which it ought to flourish. Above all, I know the sun it must turn to if it is to be what it ought to be.

There is nothing specially Yogi about this meditation. But the ideas came to me when I was calm, relaxed and at peace, with my legs bent in the form of a lotus, and my inward eye was firmly fixed on a flower, any flower seen or imagined. They came of themselves. And be sure that similar ideas will come naturally to you after a few weeks or a few months of visualization and localization exercises.

You see the procedure. More particularly, you see the purpose: to focus my soul, my mind, on a single subject; centre my thoughts, and especially my subconscious, on simpler and simpler ideas, on more and more spiritual ideas; to prepare myself to embrace, in the depths of my heart, and in silence, the most interior of all my possessions: God.

Attention; concentration; identification; you will certainly not reach perfection in these exercises in a few days or a few weeks. Let me ask you to put your trust in the method. What it does, as you will have understood, is to liberate your intellect and undertake the re-training of certain powers which lie dormant in you. It is a matter of time. But what counts is the quality, rather than quantity, of time you devote to this task. I have said it, and I say it again (your success, health, your equilibrium too, are at stake): ten minutes, a quarter of an hour a day spent in "concentration" (in whatever form you like) — that is ample, at the beginning, at least. As the months and years go by you will do more, in the sense that your mind, made more supple, more sensitive and also more luminous, will react more quickly to the symbols, as well as the lessons, of things and events.

B. POSTURES

Exercise 41: The Pole

Place a large, rather hard, cushion against the wall (a rug folded in four will do very well). Get down on your knees and bend forward till your head is resting on the middle of the cushion (about a foot from the wall); hands encircle the temples and your fingers meet on the crown of the head. Elbows and forearms are resting on the cushion, and they form a sort of triangle on which the whole weight of the body is supported (fig. 40).

Then you have to give a little spring and balance your body against the wall. The feet leave the floor, the thighs are close up against the body and the legs are folded back on the thighs (fig. 41).

Fig. 40. "THE POLE" (Phase One)

Keep in this position a moment so as to balance yourself properly on the triangle made by your arms and hands. Try cautiously to move your body away from the wall, but if you cannot do this at the beginning it doesn't matter.

Fig. 41. "THE POLE" (Phase Two)

Then straighten your legs and thighs and bring them to the horizontal position.

All that remains now is to give another push so as to raise your legs to the vertical position. Curve your trunk and rest your legs against the wall (fig. 42).

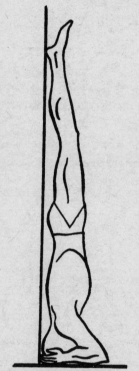

Fig. 42. "THE POLE" (Phase Three)

You will gradually have to get your legs away from the wall, first for a few seconds and then for longer and longer periods. At the same time you will have to change the position of your head and shoulders till your body is really straight like a pole, with the head downwards, in perfect balance (fig. 43).

This posture is certainly spectacular. It may seem impossible to do. No, it is merely difficult, and it marks a victory over oneself. It may be said that victory is complete

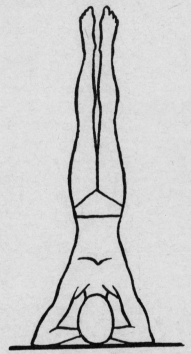

Fig. 43. "THE POLE" (Phase Four)

when you can get your feet off the floor without a jerk, almost without a jump, and when you can get into position in slow time, paying proper attention to the three positions and holding each of them a little while. Once you have taken up the position correctly, you must be able to return to the position in phase two (fig. 41), with your legs and thighs folded, then take up the vertical position again, hold your legs and thighs wide apart and so on. You must be able to get back to the starting position slowly without falling heavily; you must even be able to stretch out your legs and thighs in the horizontal position, so that they form a right angle with your trunk, a few seconds before you bring them down again with your feet on the floor. You must be able ... but I don't want to frighten you. ... Still, I have seen a good number of my disciples (young ones, it is true) bring off all these achievements; as for me, I have managed to do it, but it took me two years.

After a certain time, the fact that you find it more or less easy to take up the posture becomes a sort of test. For, I forgot to tell you, there are good and bad days for doing the *Pole*. Today, I feel I could stay upside down indefinitely. Tomorrow, as soon as I am in position, I shall feel my legs trembling, and I shall find it impossible to keep still, as perfection in this posture demands. In that case I shall not try to keep it up for more than a few seconds. I shall say: "Things will be better tomorrow," and gently bring my feet to the floor again. Prudence alone demands that you should accustom your organism gradually, and somewhat slowly, to this essential posture. From two to three seconds at the outset, you work up to ten seconds after two weeks; after a month you will be able to do thirty seconds, and so on. There comes a time when you can stay upside down on your head for five, seven or even ten minutes, and that without any inconvenience – rather the opposite – and without feeling the least discomfort or experiencing the slightest sensation of unbalance or vertigo. I have read that Pandit Nehru used to keep up this somewhat unusual posture for as long as twenty minutes every morning. . . .

Some more advice for the young, and for all beginners: if you don't manage to get "airborne" today, if after two or three attempts to raise your legs you fall back heavily, don't persist. Put off your courageous and persevering efforts till tomorrow. Your first attempts to turn upside down, and especially your apprehensions, cause, not a gentle and peaceful irrigation of the brain, but a sort of minor congestion (not a dangerous one) which will make it impossible for you to do an exercise which calls for the maximum of presence of mind and self-mastery.

The *therapeutic effects* of the *Pole* are considerable. The posture acts on the physical and the psychic organism. It promotes the circulation of the blood, relieves the heart and makes cerebral fatigue, headaches, etc., disappear. It cures haemorrhoids and relieves congestion in the sex organs. Moreover, it clarifies one's ideas and prepares one for intellectual work – hence its importance at the beginning of the day and before exercises in concentration. It combats inferiority complexes, gives self-confidence and counter-acts inhibitions and timidity. At the same time it is a factor making for humility. "If I were one day tempted", said Nehru, "to ignore or forget my origins, this exercise would remind me!"

Contra-indications. In my opinion, only those people who suffer from hypertension will have to avoid this exercise. You must not let yourself be affected by the idea that "the blood rushes to the head and then . . .". That is wrong: the blood does not rush to the brain; it merely gets there more easily, and one gland (the pineal) finds its work considerably stimulated. So follow the advice you are given: stop at the slightest sign of discomfort, don't go on if you meet with failure, confine your first attempts to a few seconds, and don't make it any longer until some months have passed. I guarantee that if you take these simple precautions you will never have any trouble. Quite the opposite!

C. RESPIRATION

Turn back to Lesson Six (p. 96). There I give you a method of preparation for the exercise of *Prānāyāma*, which holds an important place in the Yogi disciplines. Here now is the complete exercise:

Exercise 42: The complete Prānāyāma

Place the middle and index finger of the right hand on the bridge of the nose. Stop up the right nostril with the thumb.

1. Breathe *in* through the *left* nostril, counting up to 6.
2. Then at once *stop up* the left nostril with the third and little finger, keeping the right nostril closed. Holding this position count from 1 to 24.
3. Release the *right* nostril by lifting the thumb and breathe *out* counting from 1 to 12.
4. Breathe *in* immediately through the same (*right*) nostril and count from 1 to 6.
5. *Stop it up* and count from 1 to 24.
6. *Let go* of the *left* nostril and breathe *out* through it counting from 1 to 12.

You have done a complete *prānāyāma*: 6–24–12; 6–24–12, from left nostril to left nostril.

You can begin more modestly: 4–16–8; 4–16–8 or even 3–12–6; 3–12–6.

Never use force, and do the exercise in perfect calm. If you precede *prāṇāyāma* with some of the exercises, you should end up in the *Perfect Posture* and wait until your breathing and the beating of your heart are normal.

Don't overdo it: two or three *prāṇāyāmas* in the rhythm that seems most suitable are sufficient. Later you will do better, cautiously and slowly. You may even get to what the Yogis call the "slowest measure" – 12–48–24, though this performance is not at all necessary. I have got as far as that myself after four years, but only once or twice. I prefer to stick to my own rate (the one I have found best and which seems natural for me) and that is a modest 6–24–12.

Effects. The practice of *prāṇāyāma* is recommended each time an unforeseen incident or an unexpected event makes us lose our physical and psychical balance. Whenever our composure is threatened, before undergoing an examination, for instance, or when we are afraid, or feel anger rising or indignation breaking out. But the emotion must not have gone too far; it requires a certain amount of calm and the absence of any extreme anxiety to carry out this exercise.

It can also be used to relieve certain kinds of pain: while you are breathing in the way you have been told, you direct your attention to the point where the pain or the nervous affection is. The pain may not disappear at the first attempt, nor will the first *prāṇāyāmas* calm you down (you are in fact too much taken up by the operation itself; you are blocking your energies instead of liberating them). You will have to rely on habit to make this exercise seem natural to you, so that you can do it without any mental tension.

Contra-indications. If my advice is followed, and the complete *prāṇāyāma* is not undertaken until you have prepared the way for it by the breathing exercises described in the earlier lessons, there is no danger in practising it, in moderation, every morning. Too much haste, too much practice, could cause a certain lack of mental or sexual balance. Every Yogi must find his own capacity and stick to it.

Lesson Nine

THE LIFE OF A YOGI

THEORY
AND PRACTICE

Down with routine

THEORY and practice are combined in this penultimate lesson. The theory is simple: you must avoid routine. All our Yogi exercises must be carried out consciously. They must *combine* body and soul in a common effort. But this effective presence of the body in the soul can only be brought about, at least in the early days, if the *āsanas* and the breathing exercises really take up all our attention. Care must be taken that by becoming too easy, too automatic so to speak, they do not let slip the very links, between soul and body, that they were intended to create.

One method of avoiding routine (and of course we try to avoid it in connection with the exercises so that we can get rid of it in our lives) is to make the *āsanas* which have been suggested somewhat more complicated. Each time they are carried out, some new feature should be introduced: a special effort, a further step towards the perfecting of the pose (rarely obtained, except after years of practice). We are going to turn back therefore to each of the postures you have been in the habit of combining with each other since Lesson Six.

Fig. 44. "THE TRAPEZE"

Exercise 43: The Trapeze

But first practise taking up correctly a position that will serve as a starting-point for postures like the *Deep Obeisance*, or the *Backstretch*, and as intermediate postures in the *Tree* or the *Lotus*.

Hold your hands together in front of your chest. Keeping them together, and quite straight, lift them up and put them on top of your head. The arms, with the forearms and the line of the collar-bones, form a sort of trapeze. The elbows must not be facing each other but must be as far apart as possible (fig. 44).

Exercise 44: The Deep Obeisance (Variant)

First do the *Trapeze*. Keep your arms on the same vertical plane and lift your hands, still joined together, as high as you can, with your arms close to your ears. All the time, quite naturally, you are breathing deeply. Then, keeping your hands together, you bend forwards till you can touch the ground with the tips of your fingers. At the same moment, you open your arms and clasp your ankles or grip the back of your feet, with your forearms placed alongside the legs. Bring your head up to your knees (fig. 45).

Fig. 45. "THE DEEP OBEISANCE" (Variant)

Note that success depends on the amount of stretching done by the spinal column, especially the lumbar vertebrae. So direct your attention to these vertebrae, already more supple as a result of the exercises in the first eight lessons. Put up with the pain in your legs, which are stretched to the utmost. Don't be alarmed if you are attacked by a slight vertigo as you get up. That will go. Breathe deeply (it is scarcely necessary for me to recommend this) once you are standing up again.

Fig. 46. "THE TREE" (Variant)

Exercise 45: The Tree (Variant)

You will see it at once: this variation consists of placing your foot, not, this time, sole against thigh, but with the sole firmly in front of the thigh. Your attempts – and successes – at taking up the *Perfect* posture have made your legs more supple and your ankles less stiff. The sole of the foot is turned uppermost and the ankles supported as near as possible to the groin (fig. 46).

In the early stages you will have to bend forward to catch hold of your foot and bring it up to the position indicated. It will also be necessary, no doubt, to carry the bent knee a little to the rear (to prevent the foot slipping).

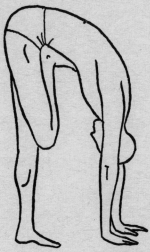

Fig. 47. "THE BENT TREE"

Exercise 46: The Bent Tree

Get into a properly balanced position (see previous exercise), raise your arms and then ... you lean slowly forward with your arms stretched right out. You bend and try to put both hands flat on the ground (fig. 47), as in the *Deep Obeisance* (Phase Two, p. 38).

At first, just try to touch the ground with the tips of your fingers.

Your foot remains firmly in place against the thigh on which it is resting heavily. Your head is getting as close as it can to the knee of your outstretched leg; that is, assuming, as in Exercise 44, that there is a complete stretching of the lumbar vertebrae.

The difficulties you encounter in taking up this position and holding it (not more than a second or two at first) will be a measure of your lack of balance or, to put it more clearly, your need to balance yourself. When, after a number of unsuccessful attempts, you manage to do it, you will feel, I have no doubt, that you have gained a victory over yourself. You will get there, as I have got there, in spite of my fifty-four years!

Fig. 48. "THE TRIANGLE" (Variant)

Exercise 47: The Triangle (Variant)

This method of doing the *Triangle* is to be combined with the first (pp. 96–98). After turning to the right and then the left and bending the trunk, return to the starting position: stand up, feet apart, arms in the horizontal position, continuing the line of your shoulders. Without twisting, bend the trunk to the right till it is at a right angle to the line of your legs and the *right* hand is touching the toes of your *right* foot (fig. 48). Stand up again, breathe in, and do the same movement to the *left*. It is more difficult to do than the first method. The head swings slightly and turns towards the ceiling.

Exercises 48, 49, 50: The Snake, the Bent Bow, the Dolphin

These postures do not admit of any variations; but there are more and less correct ways of doing them.

So far as the *Snake* (Exercise 3, p. 23; Exercise 9, p. 41) is concerned, watch that your stomach stays firmly on the ground; rely on your hands as little as possible when you get up again; this manoeuvre should be carried out by the spinal column, especially the lumbar vertebrae. On this point there is almost infinite room for improvement.

As for the *Bent Bow* (Exercise 21), the more you manage to raise the trunk, the more you do it by using the vertebrae and not the feet pulling against the hands, the more correct and perfect this posture will be.

Since the *Dolphin* (Exercise 4) is scarcely more than an intermediate posture, it calls for no remarks.

Exercise 51: The Full Backwards Bend

One variation consists of sitting down, not this time on your heels or between your heels (Exercise 29), with the tips of your toes touching, but with the buttocks planted firmly on the ground between the feet, which are wide apart. Your knees are equally wide apart and the thighs pressing down on the legs. You do not hollow the back or throw back the head: you let yourself go backwards in the supine position, the head and shoulder muscles well stretched out and also the vertebrae of the neck.

The posture is fairly hard to take up because it imposes the maximum amount of stretching on the thighs.

Exercise 52: *The Backstretch*

This exercise (see Exercise 18, p. 56) can be made a bit more complicated like this: Instead of grasping your feet with your hands, and exerting a strong pull on your toes, place the forearms alongside the legs, on the ground. It calls for greater effort. The back is stretched from side to side as well as from top to bottom. The head must touch the knees, and even touch the ground between the knees, which are wide apart. In Exercise 23 (p. 68) I have suggested a *Pubic Stretch* which will prepare the way for this variation of the *Backstretch*.

Exercises 53, 54: *The Candle and the Plough*

We already have several variations of these two postures (see combined Exercises 26 and 27, p. 82). So far as the *Candle* is concerned, the hardest consists of raising the legs almost to the vertical position (after doing the *Plough*) *without using the hands to support the trunk* at the shoulder-blades. The arms remain stretched out on the ground. The whole effort is concentrated on the spinal column (see fig. 49). In the *Plough*, try to get the legs as far back as possible. Once the trunk is upside down, bend your knees and make them touch the ground on each side of your ears. Your head is encircled by the lower part of the thighs. It's a bit hard to do. Young people manage it fairly easily and so do women, in general. You must not force it. You can

Fig. 49. "THE CANDLE" (Variant)

Fig. 50. "THE PLOUGH" (Variant Two)

get some help from your arms, at first, if you place them in
the same position as in the ordinary *Candle*: the hands push
against the shoulder-blades. Perfection would demand a
recoil resulting from the accentuation of this thrust, and
we should find ourselves on our knees, trunk upright.

Exercise 55: The Lotus (*Variants*)

This posture already represents, for the average European,
a veritable *tour de force*. Is it possible to make it more complicated, more difficult? Yes, undoubtedly! Here are two
symbolic postures (*Yoga-Mudra*, as the Indians call them –
variants of Exercise 39, p. 116) which are used especially for
prolonged meditation.

Variant One

Once your legs are crossed, with each foot resting on the
opposite thigh, join your hands together, do the *Trapeze*,
and raise your arms as high as you can above your head.

You concentrate on a point in front of you, or you direct
your gaze towards the end, or better still, the bridge, of
your nose. (This means you have to squint, but there is no
difficulty about that. On the contrary!) So your eyes are
converging towards a point near at hand. Stop as soon as
you feel the least fatigue.

You are advised to hold your breath as long as you can.
Then you breathe out gently and start breathing normally,
but very slowly, again. You conclude by bending forward
with your arms stretched right out till your hands touch
the ground. Your seat must not leave the ground. There is
an elongation, or more exactly a distension, of the dorsal
vertebrae.

Variant Two

Here is another and more difficult *Yoga-Mudra*. Starting-point: the *Lotus*. You get your trunk right back as in the *Full Backwards Bend*. You place your hands on your thighs, or, better still, on your feet. You relax.

Both postures are "dynamizing", energetic and elevating. In the first, you concentrate naturally on the pineal gland (in the middle of the forehead) or you evoke joyful, encouraging, optimistic thoughts. In the second, the solar plexus, on a level with the pit of your stomach, must be the object of your thought. At the same time you evoke the idea of strength, virile or spiritual.

Exercise 56: The Prānāyāma

I take it that you are now accustomed to this somewhat odd but very beneficial method of breathing. Here is a more perfect way of doing it: when you have filled your stomach with air (this is just a manner of speaking; it means: when you have filled the lower part of your lungs, and the diaphragm is pressing against the intestines), go on breathing until you have filled your chest with air as well (that is, first the middle, then the upper part of the lungs). To do that, you have to slightly contract the muscles of the stomach and raise first your ribs and then your collar bone. In this way you will soon reach the rhythm 12–48–24. But never strain yourself.

This has the following results:

1. The stomach is quite hollow, and the diaphragm rises as high as it can to expel as much as possible of the air from the lungs.

2. The diaphragm gently subsides, the stomach fills out and the lower part of the lungs becomes filled with air.

3. The stomach becomes slightly hollow, the chest is raised and the middle of the lungs receives the maximum amount of pure air.

4. The collar bones are raised and the shoulders with them: air comes into the upper part of the lungs. It is at this stage that both nostrils are stopped up. When you breathe out, your shoulders drop, your chest contracts and your stomach becomes hollow. And the cycle starts again. That is the true *prānāyāma*.

When you are holding your breath, imagine the vital force (the *prānā*) passing from plexus to plexus (from *chakra* to *chakra*, as the Indians say): from the sacral plexus (where the vital energy of every man is stored) the same energy passes to the hypogastric plexus, and then to the solar plexus; from there it rises to the cardiac plexus and then to the pharyngeal plexus; at the moment when you let go of one nostril to breathe out completely, imagine this energy coming into your brain and radiating throughout your being, stimulating all the glands. This exercise is particularly recommended for those who suffer from over-pronounced erotic desires. The "imaginative" rise of what the Indians call the *Kundalini*, masculine energy, sexual energy, is not a myth. But it takes for granted a certain habit of Yogi concentration and the practice of the "localization" exercises which are called for in Lesson Six.

Lesson Ten

SUMMARY

I SHOULD like to conclude by planning for you as complete a programme of life as I can. I assume, obviously, that during the course of the previous lessons you have come to the conclusion that Yoga, true Yoga, removed from its more or less magical and esoteric context, can play a great part in your existence; that it is a form of *asceticism*, and one adapted to your temperament and also to your aspirations as a man and as a Christian. I assume that you have thoroughly understood the object of this asceticism (you can make sure of this by reading and re-reading Lessons Five and Six) and that you have decided to make your daily exercises the instrument of a real development, as much on the spiritual plane as on the natural. Let me first tell you that it would be dangerous to give up completely the practice of Yoga after you have devoted yourself to it for a certain time. Yoga creates in us certain habits: it refines our nature as men; it elevates us; it makes us grow. To give it up is to fall back again. . . . Certainly, if you want to keep "in good condition" from a Yogi point of view, it is not necessary, still less indispensable, to keep to the letter of the programme I am planning for you; you need only keep to a part, a small part, of this programme, but how-

ever little you do, stay faithful to Yoga, and do at least
something of what I venture to advise here.

I. TWO SESSIONS OF YOGA A DAY

Let your day be marked by two series of exercises; two
series or two sessions, different in character and value: a
session of hard work in the morning; a session of relaxation
in the evening.

In the Morning

Not when you get up: as a general rule, it is difficult to
do most of the exercises on rising. You are too bleary-eyed.
The muscles are lazy and the mental faculties lazier still.
After a shower or a bath, and also a cup of tea or weak
coffee, some people feel in better form. So much the better.
Others can leave this session till the first free moment – but
obviously before breakfast or a certain time afterwards.

You should select rather hard exercises – those, if possible,
which make all the glands and a good part of the muscles
work.

Begin with the *Pole* (Lesson Eight) and keep it up for
several minutes, but stop as soon as you feel you are losing
your balance.

Then do the *Deep Obeisance* (Variant One, if possible:
Lesson Nine, p. 138), the *Triangle* (Lessons Six, p. 96, and
Nine, p. 143), the *Tree* (Variant One, Lesson Nine, p. 140),
and even the *Bent Tree* (Lesson Nine, p. 141), the *Snake*
(Lessons Two, p. 41, and Nine, p. 143), the *Dolphin* (Lesson
One, p. 25), the *Full Backwards Bend* with the *Folded Leaf*
(Lesson Six, p. 98).

These six or seven exercises will take you perhaps ten

minutes; and you will have irrigated your brain, the pineal gland, the thymus, the thyroid, the suprarenal glands, the sexual glands, the rachides and made them work.

Then get into one of the squatting positions which are familiar to you (Lesson Seven, pp. 110 ff.); let go the muscles of your face, your arms, your hands; relax. You should have a certain feeling of well-being. "Place" your eyes on something (Lesson Seven) or concentrate (Lesson Eight). Five minutes, ten minutes, if you have the time to spare. That may be enough. Some will voluntarily prolong these moments of silent prayer.

Of course, you can choose other postures for yourself (the *Plough* [Lesson Five], for instance, the *Backstretch* [Lesson Three] or the *Pubic Stretch* [Lesson Four]) and also carry out some *prāṇāyāmas*. Two or three exercises well done, but kept up for a few moments, make an excellent formula. Feel your way for a bit and make your selection. From time to time introduce a variation (beware of routine!).

Take advantage of the absolute calm that descends on you to *pledge your day*. This is the moment to accept, to will, all that is going to happen to you. I am sure that within a week you will feel the effect of this on your day's work, however burdened you are.

In the Evening

The evening session could take place when you go to bed at night, or even when you come home from work. The idea is to prepare yourself for sleep, to calm down completely; to get rid of all your anxieties so as to make the coming night, and even the last hours of the day, a real means of recuperation.

Select the postures of relaxation that suit you. I would suggest a combination of the various *Candles* and *Ploughs* described in Lesson Five, p. 82, concluding with the balancing exercise (fig. 29). You can also profitably do the *Back-stretch* (Lesson Three, p. 56) and make it a little more complicated like this: sit down with your legs stretched out in front of you and wide apart; bend one of them and bring the foot under the opposite buttock, with the heel pushed well into the hollow of the groin. Raise your arms and bend slowly forwards as far as you can till your forehead is close to the knee of the leg that has been kept stretched out. Hold your breath for a few seconds or more and sit up again. Then start again with the other leg.

After that the posture of *Relaxation* (Lesson Four, p. 70) is indicated. And sleep will come by itself; really restful sleep.

You can also rest content with doing the *Pole* (Lesson Eight, p. 128) – an excellent exercise for our purposes.

Do not be surprised or alarmed if you do not manage, even after six months' or even a year's practice, to carry out all the exercises in these two daily sessions of action and relaxation. And do not lose heart if you cannot carry out this programme *every day*. This is my advice to you: do something in the morning and something in the evening in the spirit I have indicated. From time to time shut yourself up, however inconvenient this might be, for a complete session in which you take time to carry out, each time better than the last, practically all the postures in this course. After seven years, I still, from time to time, do a session in which I pretend I am still a novice, and when it comes to an end I feel tired. You must always try. . . .

2. MEANWHILE...

Do not forget certain Yogi practices. I happen to work, read or write in the *Perfect* or *Hero* postures. That is a performance which is not accessible to everybody and difficult to achieve in our Western world.

Relax whenever you can: when you are working in your office, in the fields, anywhere. Learn how to stop and rest your eyes on things, how to listen, touch, be moved, how to let something pleasant make its impression on you.

Walk in the eastern manner whenever possible: quite straight, hands open, palms to the front. Make your step rhythmic and be really aware of the fact that you are walking. When you are going upstairs, put your heel on the step first, and then the whole foot. This is much less tiring than going up on your toes. Pay attention to the expansion and contraction of the muscles and tendons in your legs.

Two or three times during the day give a thought to your breathing, but don't tire yourself unnecessarily by, for instance, repeated *prāṇāyāmas* which could be prejudicial to your health.

Notice the way you are hardening to cold, and be firm about dispensing with unnecessary clothes and undergarments. Let your skin breathe freely; there is no need to smother yourself with clothes. If need be, warm yourself up with breathing exercises. That will stop you running for a coat.

Whatever you do, do it carefully and do it well, really putting yourself into your work. The humblest form of toil, the most mechanical, the most idiotic, can be made interesting and turned into relaxation. Banish from your daily life expressions like "how tiresome this is" and "what a bore" and other quite natural and human reactions. Things will go better on some days than others. . . . What a lot of factors can intervene! It is up to you to neutralize them.

3. DIET

Just a few words.

Do we have to accept the views of the Indian Swamis and cut out all flesh foods? The Indians – especially the Hindus – only do so on account of the respect they profess for everything that lives. (But doesn't a plant live? Hasn't it a soul, in the sense in which Hindu philosophy understands this word?) They are vegetarians by religious conviction. I do not think we ought to follow them on this ground, even if other motives incite us to a more sober form of nourishment.

Let everyone do what he likes, and above all what he can. I have got into the way of fasting practically every day; my morning session of gymnastics is my breakfast (air nourishes). I take only a minimum amount, therefore, of solid food. But I drink a lot during the morning: water or weak tea. It is all beneficial as a filter for the body.

In this sphere try to adopt certain habits that experience will have shown you are beneficial.

4. NOW AND AGAIN A DAY OF SILENCE

All the masters of the spiritual life recommend this practice: a day of absolute silence, at long and, if possible, regular intervals. A "day of recollection"!

"Reinforce fasting by silence. Do not address a word to

anyone on these days. If people speak to you, answer them with a gesture, or, if you are obliged to do so, in writing. No one can know what benefit this practice can be until he has tried it. Of all austerities this is the most soothing to the mind, like wool to the body, making a nest of the body's own heat" – Lanza del Vasto, *Principes et préceptes d'un retour à l'évidence* (Paris, 1945), p. 53.

Usually the only way we can keep silence is to escape from our environment, get away from it all. Surely we all can, at least once in a while? Instead of a day of so-called relaxation in town, a day of tiring, exhausting spectacles, try a day's walking on your own. Start before breakfast and take some bread with you. Look for some quiet and lovely places where you will really find pleasure in letting your eyes rest on the scenery; leave your everyday work and worries behind you. "Today I shall walk. Today I shall keep silent!" A wonderful opportunity to do a complete session of Yoga in the open air, far from mankind and far from noise.

5. AVOIDING AN EASY LIFE

Or, if you prefer, routine. In Lesson Nine, I put you on your guard against certain practices which make the postures so easy that they are in danger of yielding no fruit. The same routine can insinuate itself into our lives and turn our most elevating practices into a sort of triviality. To be a Yogi is to avoid the commonplace; it is to mark what one does with the benefit of one's presence, "being effectively and efficaciously present" in what one does: the passing of the man into the work he carries out; "the living mark of a beating heart on a deed done, a word spoken, anything done or expressed" (cf. Lesson Seven). Yoga exercises make life easier for us; that is in any case one of their objects. Look at the first lessons again. But if they bring us peace, if, by their nature, they make us gentler, they do not, let me say, dispense us from any effort to reach *perfection* – thanks to that gentleness, thanks to that profound peace – in what we have to *do* in our capacity as men and Christians. Thanks to them, we are ourselves, we possess ourselves; our three powers (body, soul and spirit) work together in substantial unity. But this unity, this "joining" (*Yoga*), must be expressed in another unity, that of *love*. The Yogi is a man who loves, who knows how to love; who looks around him with sympathy; who tries to see a little as God himself sees and to act always with love in consequence.

And it is perhaps in the sphere of love, of lively sympathy, that the easier life that Yoga, through the practice of Yoga, brings with it can find itself wanting and fail to achieve its object. I have known Yogis who ceased to practise, at least regularly, the day they felt in better condition and freed from certain impediments. A fatal gesture! Some have ended up feeling worse than before. Yoga has no end. It opens up a world of infinite perfectibility. It makes life easier only so that we can utilize it, and realize ourselves, more effectively.

So never give up your new life. When you devote yourself to Yoga, it is rather like vowing yourself to the religious life, or to the ordinary Christian life. You are introducing into your existence a principle of amendment, conversion if you like, and you have no right, so to speak, ever to give it up.

Our wonderful world lacks Christians because it lacks

men. A Christian system of Yoga aims at re-peopling the earth with Christians who are perfectly human. Have you heard the call? And if so, are you ready to respond?

It is because I think the answer is "yes" that I have worked out this admittedly austere programme; but who would build his life with trifles?

Appendix I

NOTES AND EXPLANATIONS

1. Can we dispense with a guru?

MANY people hesitate to get involved in the mysteries of Yoga without the help of an instructor, or a *guru*, as he is called.[1] They are not wrong in this attitude. Although the majority of Yoga exercises present no danger, they become dangerous, even to a man in good health, if they are practised injudiciously or to excess. What about invalids? Those who suffer from pulmonary, kidney, heart or liver trouble or from other afflictions of a similar kind, should only take up Yoga with enlightened, but not extreme, caution. Some of the exercises they will have to avoid, as well as some of the breathing exercises, and only go on with *āsanas* so far as they can be shown to be without danger to their general condition. "Experience", says Yesudian (*Sport et Yoga*, p. 130), "shows that the man who observes, however little, the reactions of his own organism very soon begins to feel instinctively which exercises are doing him good and which can do him harm." This remark by a qualified master of Yoga will reassure the timid. It does not mean that the presence of an experienced instructor may be found to be unnecessary, either

[1] See page 18.

158

for them or for others. But this instructor does not have to be a kind of medicine man whom you go and consult quite often and who takes your pulse, so to speak, at each session.

If some need supervision, and pretty close supervision at that (young people and invalids will be dealt with later), most men with common sense and most well-balanced women can launch out into Yoga with a good handbook, though they will have to follow carefully all the instructions it gives. The *Swamis*, the Indian masters, used to proclaim loudly that Yoga, their Yoga, was impracticable for Europeans without the supervision of a proper *guru*, but that is no longer true. It has been possible to bring Yoga, as tested by Europeans, within the range of the many, and the intelligent and prudent use of Yoga practices has permitted the selection of exercises which are really without danger if they are taken up as directed and in a prudent rhythm. Once you have got hold of a handbook, you will have to make a strict rule to follow all its precepts. If it is a question of lessons or a "course" spread out over a definite number of weeks, you must take care not to rush through it too quickly. Especially in the matter of rhythmic breathing and breath control, for it can be dangerous to try to run before you can walk, and it may lead to a certain disturbance of the biological rhythm or even a disastrous disintegration of the psychical structure.

But though it foresees a good deal, a manual cannot cater for everything. Even the prudent adept may find himself face to face with eventualities resulting from the release of certain of his energies; he may be in the grip of inner crises and find no explanation or cure for them in the handbook. In such cases you can always turn to the author of the book who will always be ready to explain things to a would-be disciple.[1] Moreover, it is to be hoped that some kind of Yogi circles or brotherhoods will be formed here and there where adepts can meet and share their experiences and find, if not masters, at least more advanced adepts who are in a position to give advice as well as encouragement.

Now let me come back to the question of young people and invalids. I have often been asked: "What is the earliest age at which you can advise a person to take up Yoga?" I reply: "As soon as the child or youth is in a position to treat Yoga as a discipline and not as a collection of spectacular acrobatics." At twelve? Perhaps. Fifteen or sixteen? Certainly! If the father and mother are followers of Yoga themselves, they will become the instructors of their son or daughter. In grammar schools and secondary schools, in gymnasia and other educational establishments, even in rehabilitation centres, some of the Yoga exercises can be added to the ordinary physical culture course – one or two at first, then more later. Yoga has such an educational and formative value that it would really be a pity to deprive the young of its undeniable benefits. But caution is necessary. There is a risk that a young man may get a little intoxicated by the initial results of Yoga, may go off the deep end and lose all sense of moderation (especially with regard to the respiratory exercises). The remedy is the formation of Yoga clubs where joint sessions will be held under the supervision of an "old hand". The adepts should also be able to speak in confidence to someone about the repercussions of the Yoga exercises on their moral, even their organic, life (this need not be a priest).

So far as religious communities are concerned, it hardly

[1] Fr Déchanet's address is: Monastère Saint-Benoît, Kansenia, Katanga.

seems possible nowadays for Fathers Superior and Mothers
Superior to be ignorant of Yoga. A candidate for the
monastic life or a postulant who has practised Yoga in the
world must be able to continue with his exercises in freedom, though unobtrusively. I must stress this need for
discretion: example is contagious, and the fortunate bene-
ficiary of Yogi disciplines will always be somewhat tempted
to communicate his experience to others and pass on the
benefits of it to a colleague who needs it. It is for superiors
and novice mistresses to show understanding, and authorize
Yoga, while taking care that the adepts do not set themselves
up as a sort of "caste" in the house. ... I know abbeys
where a quiet room, out of sight of the inquisitive, is reserved
for young monks who wish to practise Yoga. It is only
available at certain times. From time to time, during the
course of or on the occasion of a collective session, an "old
hand", for the benefit of the others, runs through the rules
that should regulate a sensible and profitable session.

Invalid cases are more difficult. No one who suffers from
heart trouble can take up Yoga. But I know some cardiac
cases whose condition has improved considerably as the
result of the prudent but persevering practice of Yoga. A
chest case already on the way to recovery will find the
moderate and progressive practice of the postures and the
breathing exercises a far from negligible stimulant from the
physical, and especially from the moral, point of view. A
person whose bone structure, especially the spinal column,
is not in perfect condition will not be able to undertake the
"upside down" postures (the *Pole*, the *Candle*, the *Plough*)
without extreme care. In general, any organic defect, any
functional trouble, calls for reservations, but not for total
abstinence. The doctor's advice must be followed, but it is

to be hoped that doctors are well up on the subject and in a position to recommend Yoga to their patients.

In fact, the watchwords for invalids, as for people in good health, are discretion, caution; gradual initiation; a little, done properly; scrupulous care in following the advice given in the handbooks; and if necessary recourse to a man of experience, an enlightened *guru*. There is reason to hope that such men will become less and less rare.

2. *We can say . . .*

In certain but rare cases the remedy is worse than the disease. The very exercises that by their nature are intended to restrain the more or less untimely manifestations of precocious sexuality are the very ones which, in the early stages, may unwittingly be the cause of quite contrary phenomena (a strong erection, or even an emission).[1] Either the Yogi novice will take these unexpected effects for what they are – accidents without significance (and of course without sin – like those that may be caused by swimming, riding or even, for that matter, just having a bath), which will soon cease to happen; or else his blissful astonishment, his scruples, may be succeeded or even replaced by a secret pleasure in them. But there is no reason to exaggerate the danger of incidents of this kind. So if a young man who masturbates asks our advice, let us ask him whether he is looking for a cheap counterweight or an easy remedy for the lack of balance from which he is suffering; or whether, on the other hand, he has decided to introduce Yoga into his life as a form of discipline. If the answer is "yes", encourage him, though you may have to keep a more or less sharp eye on him, as the case may be.

[1] See also p. 51.

There are no fixed or absolute rules in this field. Nevertheless, anyone who suffers from a certain morbid phobia against the body, or sexuality in general, will be advised against Yoga. Yoga wards off pathological conditions of this kind. It does not cure them or release a man from them until a fairly advanced stage has been reached.

3. Occult powers (see page 90)

Is there a master of prayer who has not put his disciples on their guard against the danger of confusing certain effects, certain by-products, of prayer (ecstasy, infused recollection, spiritual euphoria) with prayer itself? How many pseudo-mystics, too, have come to grief after a search for certain ecstatic or paranormal phenomena, natural, but extraordinary fruits of precise methods of prayer and meditation?

The masters of Yoga show themselves in general to be as prudent and circumspect as the Christian masters in face of certain effects of Yoga, and in particular of the *occult powers* which the somewhat over-enthusiastic practice of certain exercises, notably the *Mudras* (symbolic postures lasting for hours at a time), undoubtedly confer on their adepts. To say that they are harmless is to say too little: these exercises, beneficial if practised in moderation and with discretion, aim, in traditional Yoga, the Yoga of India, at nothing less than the reversal in the Yogi of the normal play of vital forces, the breaking up (through the mutation of the psycho-somatic structure of the human condition) of the natural state of man. Immobility of body leads, under certain conditions, to stability of soul. Controlled and rhythmical breathing assists clear thinking. Concentration re-trains and fortifies the intellect. But pursued in accordance with the strict rules of the Yogi, practised for hours at a time, and so monopolizing a man's whole life, these exercises lead to a veritable ontological mutation, a liberation from the ordinary laws of life, a liberation which, we are told, is a real "transcendence of the human condition", a sort of death to profane (i.e. natural) existence "constituted by the law of unlimited conditioning" and a "rebirth into an unconditioned, that is to say, perfectly free and autonomous, existence" (cf. E. Eliade, "Expérience sensorielle et expérience mystique chez les primitifs", in *Etudes Carmélitaines*, 1954, p. 89). If the exercises do not lead to madness, it is due to the prudence of the *gurus*. A judicious allocation of work no less than a gradual preparation for each session (which should include a mental and biological approach characteristic of the Indian disposition) cause the disciple to progress gradually to a transcendent state of life. The manifestations of ordinary life are neither suppressed nor sublimated; they are reversed. The Yogi, for example, is not merely in control of his sexual energy: he is also capable of arresting the seminal emission. He even claims to be able to "make his semen return to its source", by which is meant that he can return the product of his genital glands to his blood. This phenomenon, which occurs of necessity and unconsciously in any chaste man, part of whose seminal fluid is reabsorbed into his organism, is operated freely and consciously by the Yogis, they claim, by the act of their will. It is a fact. Another well-known phenomenon of a quite different kind is the power to control one's heart-beats, to increase their rhythm or slow them down, even make them imperceptible.

These paranormal powers (plus many others of a more marvellous kind, like clairvoyance, thought-reading, magical heat, ubiquity) are not an aim, above all not *the* aim pursued by the Yogi. They are at the very most a sign: a sign of death, a sign of rebirth; death to profane, limited existence, conditioned by the world of illusions (*Maya*) and bounded by that collection of aspirations and needs that make up the "me" ("I" eat, "I" drink, "I" sleep, "I" walk, "I" love, and so on); rebirth to some kind of preternatural existence, in liberty, autonomy and an accentuated consciousness of the self – that "God who is more me than I am", a good Yogi could say.

However, there exists in India and outside India a real and dangerous attraction in Yoga to the *Sidhis* or occult powers. The wisest *gurus*, while rejecting the illusions of fakirism and the magic of tantrism, cannot resist the temptation to allude to them and hold them out as a desirable fruit of Yogi practices. This is what Yesudian says (in *Sport et Yoga*, p. 175):

Western medical science has confirmed that our brains contain certain nervous centres which the average man does not use. In such people they remain dormant, and medical science has not, so far, found any rational explanation for their existence. But these nervous centres are perfectly well known to the Hindu Yogis who, thanks to progressive research over thousands of years, have discovered the way to arouse and stimulate them. All the Yogi exercises (especially the *Pole* and the *Candle*) have this tendency, whether we like it or not, to arouse these centres and put us in possession of faculties the existence of which is generally unsuspected. . . .

These faculties comprise telepathy, clairvoyance, knowledge of the past and future, and other powers we

call "occult". Anyone who takes up Hatha-Yoga
seriously acquires them. The sceptic himself can be convinced if he will have the time and the patience to allow
the nerve centres in himself to develop beyond their usual
extent.

There is no cause for alarm if a Christian Yogi finds
himself more intuitive, more clairvoyant, if he amazes
people by his wonderful powers of memory, if he
astonishes them by his powers of endurance, and even if
he experiences, from time to time, some paranormal powers
(for my own part I have noticed some curious, very curious,
presentiments, like premonitions). If he takes pleasure in
these effects or by-products of Yoga, if he desires them
intensely, if he makes them the object of his exercises, that
is another thing. His *aim* is rotten to the core and cannot
lead to anything but bitter disillusion.

Appendix II

SYMBOLIC POSTURES
AND PERSONAL LITURGY

THE Indian Yogis give the name of *Mudras* or *Bandhas* to a certain number of symbolic postures, and speak highly of the effects they have on the organic, psychical and spiritual life. These postures, they say, are "dynamizing", energetic or elevating. I have mentioned several of them (cf. Lesson Nine, pp. 146 ff.). I should like to put forward here certain corporal attitudes, based on Yoga or Yoga-inspired symbolic postures, which you will associate with the evocation of spiritual thoughts and ideas – and which are capable of producing definitely religious states of mind within you.

I

Stand up very straight, but not stiff, facing East (where the sun rises), with your stomach flat (neither drawn in nor sagging), shoulders slightly back, arms falling naturally; alert and relaxed.

Breathe in and out several times and then, while breathing in deeply, raise your arms and hands (palms to the front) a little in front of and above you. There is no question of raising them to the vertical position (in a graceless "hands up" position), but hold your arms up lightly so that your hands, held open naturally, are more or less (the choice is yours) on the level of your head.

You will soon see what I mean if I tell you that in making this gesture your thought will be "Father!" You will evoke your "Father who is in heaven". To him, your creator, the source of all energy, divine and human, you lift up your arms, you hold out your hands, in an attitude of reverence, wonder and love. "Father, our Father." And all your being goes out to him – a "projection" which responds to *him* who constantly approaches *you*.

After a little while stretch out your arms horizontally in line with your shoulders, your hands open and facing upwards towards heaven.

Your thought is: "Son". You evoke the *incarnate Word*, God of God, Light of Light, very God of very God. You evoke our Lord on the tree of the cross and, like him, you offer yourself in a gesture of self-abandonment as well as acceptance (Your will be done, O Lord).

Again after a little while, listen to your heart beating and unite it with his.

Then bring your arms together and hold out your hands in the form of a cup, as if to receive the grace and love which are offered to you. You should now be thinking: "Holy Spirit", "Love", "Gift of God".

You conclude this personal liturgy by joining your hands and bowing to say the *Gloria* or simply a sincere "Amen".

This symbolic posture can also be carried out in the *Kneeling Position* or in one of the squatting positions described in Lesson Seven.

It can very advantageously be included in the course of a complete session, between the *Tree* or the *Triangle* and the *Snake* posture; before or after the *Full Backwards Bend* and so on. It can serve as an introduction or conclusion to a whole series of exercises. Finally, just calling it to mind during the day can and ought to renew in us the state of mind it created or of which it was the expression.

II

Take up the *Kneeling Position* (or the *Perfect* posture or the *Lotus*). Place your hands on your thighs or palms uppermost in front of you. Relax by breathing deeply several times. Then lower your gaze to your palms; concentrate on them and give yourself up to ideas like these:

Your hands are you; the you that acts and works. Not only are they the instruments of the brain for carrying out very precise tasks, typically human tasks (writing for instance); but also they are very often the brain's delegates for carrying out delicate missions, and in them, too, they are very characteristic of man. What my eyes cannot tell me I ask of my hands, through the sensitive tips of my fingers. My hands explore, touch, see. My hands gather together (all that delicate handling can bring me). My hands give. Nothing, not even a look of tenderness, can take the place of a mother's gesture of love when she lays her hand gently on her child's head. And the warmest and most effective benedictions are imparted by the laying on of hands.

My hands are me. My personality is written on them (as it is written, without any conscious thought of mine, in the characters traced by the pen between my fingers). In my palm there is a whole network of lines in which the hills and valleys form a picture not so much of my fate (though hand-reading of the genuine kind, without the nonsense that sometimes goes with it, is no myth) as of my activity as a man, my incommunicable self.

My eyes are contemplation. My hands action.

Lift up your hands. The *right* hand is more industrious and more communicative; the *left* hand is more representative of your passive, withdrawn self. Raise them breast-high, as high as your throbbing heart. Let your arms hang down without stiffness, elbows on hips or even away from the body. Your forearms are held out effortlessly. And now gently draw your hands apart and let them assume a natural form. The fingers separate and are slightly curved; the palms are hollow, the left more than the right, since that is the one that receives and gathers up.

And the symbol is going to work. It is working already. Your hands are you – your subconscious took a firm hold on this idea during the previous period of concentration. They are your most profound, most natural self *in the sight of God*. In the cup of your hands your soul, freely and spontaneously offering itself to the Lord, presents itself to him, seeking to hold itself before his eyes, lie before him, bathe in his light and be penetrated by his warmth.

Is there anything you ought to say? Anything you ought to think? Should you utter a prayer? Is it necessary? Your hands speak. Let them speak. Your hands express your thoughts. Your hands symbolize your self as a creature, humbly, efficaciously open to him who alone can fill you. And perhaps your lips will open – and your eyes may be contemplating, between your receptive hands, something more than emptiness – and draw breath: *os meum aperui et attraxi Spiritum*, say the Scriptures. Or again this simple word will come to your mind: Fill, O Lord, the cup of my outstretched hands.

Another day, take up the same posture, arms and elbows held away from the body. Raise your hands to the level of your face; your fingers are stretched out, close together; only your thumbs make a fairly wide angle outwards.

And it is your *self* that surrenders: "Take, Lord, take all I have," say your outstretched hands. "My soul is there, in my hands, and all day long I will hold it out as if at arm's length for you to do as you wish with it; and all this day I will carry it, joyous and light-hearted, wherever you will."

I do not think it will take you three days to penetrate the secrets of this "personal liturgy". You will discover for yourself other ways of making your hands – or your arms – express an attitude of your soul, or else to create that attitude in yourself. If you feel weary, discouraged, repeat in secret the gesture with your two hands. If circumstances do not permit you to draw attention to yourself, then just imagine and think about it. Then you will understand the words of Scripture: "To thee in my distress I have stretched out my hands", and "In the day of my distress I sought God with outstretched hands in the night". The gestures of prayer in the Catacombs, those of the priest at the altar (unfortunately often scamped and lifeless) will at last have a meaning for you. If you are a priest, your sacerdotal attitude at Mass, in the confessional, in the pulpit, will take on a new meaning, both for you and your flock. When you lift up your hands at the Preface, it will not be in vain. During the Canon, there will be nothing hieratic, stuffy or conventional about your outstretched arms. This personal liturgy will be for you a sort of landing via which you enter the sanctuary of the Church on level ground.

The Fathers did not expect Yoga to be a means of making

the body a worthy instrument of prayer and the contemplative life. But Yoga, properly understood, ought to teach us to return to the Fathers and find again, with them, the way to God.

Index

(The *āsanas*, or postures, are in capitals)

173